THE LOVE OF
BRITAIN

THE LOVE OF
BRITAIN

Wilfrid Rolfe

❧ CONTENTS ❧

page 1: The Sussex Downs
pages 2–3: Lower Slaughter, Gloucestershire
right: Longleat House

First published in 1976 by Octopus Books Limited
59 Grosvenor Street, London W.1.
ISBN 0 7064 0528 5
Produced by Mandarin Publishers Limited
22a Westlands Road, Quarry Bay, Hong Kong
Printed in Hong Kong

🙰 INTRODUCTION 🙰

When I was asked to write an introduction to this book my first reaction was one of enthusiasm. This Nation needs books like this. There cannot be too many.

Of recent years it has become the fashion for the British to belittle Britain. Unlike our ancestors we look at our country with a jaundiced eye. Too often we consider only the shortcomings, most of which are material. The one thing we can all beat the drum about is that which we have in abundance – our Heritage. That's what this book is all about and a very good thing too; the one colossal blessing we can all enjoy is the natural scene about us.

Because of the 'tightness' of these Isles one never needs to travel far to discover fascinating corners in each of its regions, its villages, towns and cities. Tremendous strides have been made in recent years in the network of Tourist Information Centres, where one can obtain help and advice on the facilities in every area – beauty spots, historical monuments, stately homes, festivals, battle grounds, village crafts, museums, mountains, dales, parks, nature walks – all can be seen, often with the minimum of effort and expense.

Too often we take for granted that which is on our doorstep. It is very easy to be embarrassed by a visitor from abroad who has taken the trouble to learn more about a facet of our immediate environment than we know ourselves. It is amazing to discover that practically every foreign visitor wishes to see Stonehenge, when a good many of us have never given it a thought since our school days let alone considered that it is as much of an asset as the Grand Canyon is to the United States of America.

I was born and bred in the West Country – so naturally my heart is where my ancestors settled from choice and where, apart from the War years I have always chosen to remain. I am proud of the fact that in my own way I have managed to preserve for posterity the magnificent Elizabethan House in which I was fortunate to be born. Indeed I take pride, too, in having started the Stately Home Business so that Britain now has so many fine Houses open for the enquiring visitor to enjoy. Longleat is my consuming passion, not only the House, but the land surrounding it, the lakes, the gardens and the forests. I am delighted to see all the visitors – some of whom simply come in the evening to walk their dogs, and enjoy the unchanged view from Heavens Gate where Bishop Ken centuries ago enjoyed the view before them. These are the visitors who probably live locally and know the House well, and fall into the category of the folk who still appreciate the simple pleasures of life. They sit looking Westwards over two Counties, humming a bit, and thinking a bit, and reckoning at dusk that there really isn't anywhere to match Britain.

It seems to me that this Book is going to serve a great many useful purposes. For those of us that are a bit lethargic and slow to start, it may, by dint of the glorious photography, help to get us moving to see for ourselves that which the camera has portrayed. For the visitor to Britain it will help to decide what best to see in each of our Regions and for all who read it, let us hope it will leave us with renewed love of Britain.

Bath

6th Marquess of Bath

A PORTRAIT OF BRITAIN

A PHOTOGRAPH OF A FRIEND is always more informative than a picture of a stranger. So here, for those who do not know Britain well, are a few facts and figures that should help to give added dimensions to the photographs in this book.

In world terms the British Isles are tiny. Great Britain, which is merely the political term used for the three countries of England, Scotland and Wales, covers an area barely one-third that of the state of Texas. Now Texas may not be as big as some Texans believe but, during the First World War when the United States announced that two million soldiers were to be shipped across the Atlantic to England, there was widespread disbelief that there could possibly be room for so many additional people in 'that little dot on the map'. Little dots on world maps usually turn out to be a lot bigger when you reach them and Britain has, in fact, just about one acre of dry land for every one of its nearing sixty million inhabitants. So no visitor to Britain – and some nine million arrive each year – need fear to find standing room only. In addition, for those who do not mind getting their feet wet, there are some 600,000 acres of inland water – canals, lakes and rivers.

Even so, Britain is a very compact unit. The distance from Land's End in the far south-west to John o' Groats in the far north-east is a little under 600 miles as the 'Concorde' flies and the greatest east-west dimension is about 350 miles. Thus no place is ever very far distant from any other place – a fact which really makes it relatively easy to see a great deal of the country in a very short time.

Happily for those who love the countryside the population spread in Britain is very uneven. One third of the people live in urban areas which occupy only about three per cent of the land. To many people's astonishment there are, particularly in Wales and much of Scotland, great tracts of uninhabited and almost unvisited country, and in England itself it is not uncommon to hear of search parties looking for walkers reported missing in the wild open spaces of Dartmoor, the Lake District or the Yorkshire moors. Even around London and other big cities there are still places so rural and peaceful that foxes, deer and badgers abound and often surprise townspeople by wandering through their gardens or even, sometimes, raiding their refuse bins.

On the whole Britain's scenery does not attempt to compete in grandeur with such outsize marvels as the Grand Canyon or the Himalayas. Her speciality (though the Scottish highlands, Snowdonia and the Cumbrian lakes instantly refute it) is the man-made scene: the ordered landscape, the compact view, the happy juxtaposition of church and village green, cottage and tree, wood and hillside, house and park.

Man certainly created the towns and cities but he also fashioned much of the countryside of Britain when he carved fields out of the forest land, drained swamps and planted the hedgerows. Man-made, too, were the parks and pleasure-grounds which surround the great houses of the 'landed gentry' and which are such an agreeable feature of the British scene. The two most famous names in landscape gardening both belong to the eighteenth century – Lancelot 'Capability' Brown and Humphrey Repton. Both had an intense and instinctive feeling for the quality of English landscape: Brown the practical gardener turned artist; Repton the imaginative artist turned gardener. Economic pressures are constantly eroding these big estates and hundreds of country houses, many of real architectural merit, have been pulled down since 1945 because their owners could not afford to maintain them. Some of the more enterprising owners of the larger estates, like the Marquess of Bath at Longleat, the Earl of March at Goodwood and the Duke of Bedford at Woburn, have turned them into money-earning businesses catering for a wide spectrum of tourists and holidaymakers. Other estates have come into the hands of the National Trust and other charitable organizations dedicated to preserving Britain's treasures for the benefit of the people for all time.

Since Britain is an island and nowhere is more than 80 miles from the sea, the sea and the sea coast occupy an exceptional position in the affections and in the recreational life of her people. There can be few Britons who have never seen the sea or spent a holiday at the seaside – and what an inviting seaside it is. The waters around Britain may not be as warm as the Mediterranean (though because of the influence of the Gulf stream they never get really cold) but her beaches, bays, inlets, cliffs and rocky headlands are incomparable and rival anything that Europe can muster, while her energetic tidal system scours the coasts clean twice a day. If guaranteed warmth and sunshine could be added to the scenic splendours of the west coast of Scotland it would quickly become the world's most sought-after playground. In all, Britain has 6000 miles of coastline, again much of it preserved by the National Trust or by local authorities. The sea, which has been Britain's most formidable defence in the past, may now have lost that role, but at least it seems right that every citizen should have access to it: there is

I.

virtually no private foreshore in Britain.

Britain is singularly rich in ecclesiastical architecture and her cathedrals, mostly the concept of Norman architects, certainly excel in size and arguably in style and magnificence many of those in Europe, while the churches which are such a feature of every town and village are something of which even non-Christians are singularly proud. In them can be traced every architectural influence from pre-Saxon to the present day. One factor which has a continuous influence on everything in Britain is the climate. It greens the fields, weathers the stone, shapes the hills and ripens the crops. Every Briton claims an inalienable right to complain about the weather. King Charles I, who is credited with the remark that the English summer is made up of three fine days followed by a thunderstorm, was merely giving royal approval to the right that his subjects demanded. They complain not because the weather is necessarily bad but because it is changeable

2.

3.

4.

5.

and unpredictable. The Meteorological Office does its best and its forecasts are usually right – somewhere.

But weather conditions in Britain are so localized that their forecast may be hopelessly wrong in one place but perfectly right a few miles away. Compared with many parts of the world Britain's climate is benign: there are rarely extremes of heat or cold, hurricanes are unknown, rainfall is low in the south and east, moderate in the west and north and, contrary to Hollywood's belief that London is perpetually enshrouded, fog is experienced on fewer than five days a year on average. In the summer,

6.

1. The Yeoman Warders at the Tower of London
2. Dufton, Cumbria
3. A field of corn stooks in County Down
4. Bamburgh Castle, Northumberland
5. The 'local': an exchange of views over a beer in the pub
6. Pittenweem, Fife

because of Britain's latitude, daylight can be 18 hours long.

In spite of her political and economic problems, in spite of planning errors that have allowed industry to mar large areas of countryside, in spite of housing, roads, railways, pylons, power stations, car parks and television aerials, Britain remains a happy, green and very pleasant land full of pleasure-giving sights, sounds and scenery; a country that engenders much love and devotion especially among those who for one reason or another have had to leave her shores. There can be no country in the world which so many misty-eyed exiles fondly refer to as 'home'.

THE HIGHLANDS AND ISLANDS

A MAP OF SCOTLAND which indicates the new administrative boundaries reveals that the largest county is now called 'Highland'. It enfolds the former counties of Caithness, Sutherland, Ross & Cromarty and Inverness and is probably as near as officialdom will ever come to defining the limits of the Highlands. There are Scots who will tell you that the Highlands are nothing to do with boundaries, that they are a state of mind. That is too esoteric an attitude for most people to comprehend and those who like their definitions to be tidy if not precise are prepared to agree that everything north and west of the Caledonian Canal is Highlands.

Beyond the canal, which stretches 60 miles (96.5 km.) from Beauly Firth to Fort William, there is a world that is totally different from the rest of Britain – grander, wider, freer, older, positively primeval. And beyond the Highlands are most of Scotland's 787 islands of which more than 100 are inhabited. To the far north are the 117 islands of the Shetland group, 100 miles (161 km.) north of the 49 islands of the Orkney group. Both groups are likely to experience radical changes in their life patterns as a

Left: Eilean Donan crowns a small island where Lochs Alsh, Long and Duich meet. Attacked by the English in 1719 for sheltering Jacobites, the restored castle is now a museum and war memorial and visitors are welcome.
Above: To the remote island of Iona, off the west coast of Mull, St. Colomba came in 563 A.D. to christianize Scotland. 48 Scottish kings lie buried in the Abbey precincts.

result of the exploitation of North Sea oil, but the two are fundamentally different. In the epigrammatic words of Moray McLaren, the Orcadian is a farmer with a boat while the Shetlander is a fisherman with a piece of land. To the west the islands group themselves into the Outer and Inner Hebrides, names that have gained romantic overtones from the lilting music of sad Gaelic songs and from the legends of Bonnie Prince Charlie. Mendelssohn, too, has added an outsider's contribution with his Hebridean Overture inspired by the sight of Fingal's Cave. The Inner islands, of which Skye is the largest, are almost as mountainous as the mainland but parts of Uist and Lewis are relatively level while Tiree, the southernmost island of all, has a Gaelic nickname which means, in rough translation, 'the kingdom whose heights are lower than the waves'. Tiree is blessed with a very mild climate.

Back on the mainland there is one part of Highland county that is notably 'un-highland', the Thurso-Wick-John o' Groats triangle. Inland from the rocky and spectacular coast there are extensive tracts of uninhabited and un-inhabitable peat bogs. Here, between John o' Groats and Dunnet Head, the Queen Mother has her favourite castle-home of Mey, which she bought in 1952. Formerly known as Barrogill Castle, it was built in the sixteenth century and belonged to the Earls of Caithness. John o' Groats (named after John de Groot, a Dutchman who ran the Orkney ferry) is popularly thought of as the northernmost point of mainland Scotland, a distinction which rightly belongs to Dunnet Head which is two miles (3.2 km.) nearer the North Pole. From Dunnet Head's precipitous cliffs 300-foot (90 m.) high, a lighthouse throws its steady beam across the turbulent waters of the Pentland Firth to Hoy, Flotta (at the entrance to Scapa Flow) and Mainland Orkney.

The core of the Highlands lies to the west between Ardnamurchan and Cape Wrath where mountain and loch endlessly alternate to make scenery unmatched anywhere else on earth. And looking seawards from Ardnamurchan Point there is a view of islands that includes those schoolboy favourites Rum, Eigg and Muck as well as Coll, Tiree and, on a fine day, the Outer Hebrides. The passage north across Wester

Above: Crofters' cottages, such as these at Gearranan on the island of Lewis, are in danger of disappearing from the Scottish scene. Young people find life in Stornaway more attractive and even the older people often need to augment the small income from their crofts by hand-weaving the famous tweed that takes its name from the con-tiguous island, Harris.

Below: Stornoway, the main town and port of the Isle of Lewis, has a population of some 5000 mainly engaged in fishing and tweed-weaving. Herrings are being packed for export in this picture but there is also a big trade in lobsters. Tourism is making great progress in the island which has spectacular sandy beaches.

Right: Ben Loyal, with its four granite peaks, looms over the barren moorland that surrounds Loch Loyal. One of the most northerly mountains of Scotland, it rises to a height of 2506 feet (762 m.) out of a truly primeval landscape formed of some of the oldest rock in Britain.

Above: The Highland cattle of Scotland are rarely bred elsewhere because they are slow to mature and their milk yield is low, but they are very hardy and their milk is rich. In colour they range from straw-yellow through several shades of red to almost black. They are an exceptionally docile breed.

Left: Scotland has some of the most magnificent beaches in the world as this photograph of Traigh Seilebost in the island of Harris proves. The seas of the Outer Hebrides benefit from the warm currents of the Gulf Stream.

Above: Rising through the mists behind Loch Leathan on the east coast of Skye, the Old Man of Storr challenges climbers who find The Storr (2358 feet/719 m.) too easy. It is a 160-foot (49 m.) natural obelisk of black trap-rock first climbed in 1955. It can be seen from the road running north from Portree.

Ross involves taking either the beautiful if adventurous coast road by Loch Torridon and Loch Maree to Gairloch or crossing half the country to join the road from Inverness to Ullapool. This latter road, just before coming to Loch Broom, passes close to the Corrieshalloch Gorge where the Falls of Measach plunge 200 feet (60 m.) into the echoing depths. Ullapool is the natural centre for this area. It is a small fishing port on a promontory jutting out from the northern shore of Loch Broom.

North of Ullapool the roads, which are rapidly being widened and resurfaced to cope with the increased traffic that North Sea oil and tourism are generating, are often single tracks with passing points marked by a diamond-shaped sign on a pole.

Cape Wrath, the north-west extremity of the mainland, is not accessible by car. Durness is the nearest village and it is possible to take a ferry over the Kyle of Durness to Achemore from where, in the summer months, a minibus completes the journey to the cape. The road along the north coast gives spectacular coastal and mountain scenery for the first 40 miles (64 km.) to Tongue, but after Tongue the best of the Highlands is southward past Loch Loyal and the four-peaked Ben Loyal to Altnaharra and that other world beyond the Caledonian Canal.

MID-SCOTLAND, ARGYLL AND THE GRAMPIANS

MID-SCOTLAND is altogether too prosaic a title for all that lies south of the Great Glen and north of the Forth-Clyde basin. The grandeur of its scenery and the rich embroidery that history has stitched into its towns calls for some more resounding description. Grampians are the mountains but Grampian is the new name for the old county of Aberdeenshire and its near neighbours. The county of Argyll has also been enlarged and renamed Strathclyde. Few welcome the changes so there can be no harm in ignoring them when it is convenient. 'From Grampian to Argyll and the Isles' is one description which, while not strictly conformist, does *sound* like the clash of claymore and the shout of clansmen that once echoed from one end to another of these lovely but turbulent valleys and hills.

In Grampian, or more specifically, in Aberdeenshire the Spey, the Don and the Dee fan out to carry the melting snows of the Cairngorms through some of Scotland's most lyrical mountain and forest scenery to the shores of the moody North Sea. Between their estuaries, around the Buchan coast, there is revived seaward activity at the fishing ports of Buckie, Banff, Rosehearty, Fraserburgh and Peterhead while at Cruden Bay the cause of all the activity – North Sea oil from BP's Forties Field – has made its landfall to the south of the long, sandy bay by the famous golf links. From Aberdeen come rumours of scenes reminiscent of the California gold rush, but it is hard to believe that sturdy, steady, granite-grey Aberdeen could ever be deeply changed by anything quite as transient as an oil boom.

Inland, at any rate, the Dee still shimmers over the rocks at Braemar and Balmoral, hiding the salmon from the wading fisherman just as the heather on the moors above hides the grouse and the pine forests the deer. Westward in the Cairngorm mountains, Aviemore longs for a hard bright winter to set its ski slopes alive after the summer climbers have gone. Further south the Grampian valleys allow the rivers to widen into long, narrow lochs. Seen from the surrounding hillsides the valleys cradle them like strips of molten silver. From an elevated viewpoint between Pitlochry and Kinloch Rannoch, the 'Queen's View' down Loch Tummel must be the finest in the whole of Scotland – at least

Queen Victoria thought so and, understandably, the Scots were very quick to broadcast her enthusiasm.

The river Tummel joins the Tay below Pitlochry and flows on to Perth to form the wide Tay estuary which separates Perth and Dundee from Fife. This estuary is crossed by two famous bridges: the railway bridge which replaced the notorious 'disaster' bridge opened in 1878 and blown down in a gale the following year with the loss of 75 lives, and the modern road bridge, opened in 1966, to replace the congested but well-loved ferry. Before the Forth and Tay road bridges were opened, Fife was a somewhat aloof

Below: In a romantic setting beside the Aray where it joins the headwaters of Loch Fyne, stands Inveraray Castle, the headquarters of the clan Campbell since the fifteenth century. The present castle, the home of the Duke of Argyll, the Campbell chief, was completed in 1770. It is an early and outstanding example of the neo-Scottish baronial style. Damaged by fire in November, 1975, it is now being restored.

Right: Snow on the mountains adds exciting contrasts as this view of Stob Ghabhar (3565 feet/1085 m.) from across the waters of Loch Tulla proves. Loch Tulla is a small, remote, inland loch near the Bridge of Orchy on the road to Glencoe.

Right: The prominent mountain seen in this picture is the Pap of Glencoe (2430 feet/740 m.). It is the westernmost peak of a six-mile-long (9.7-km.) ridge, Aonach Eagach, running along the north side of Glencoe, the notorious pass where, in 1692, 40 members of the clan MacDonald were massacred by soldiers of William III's army commanded by a member of the clan Campbell, Campbell of Glenlyon. The loch in the foreground is Loch Leven, a sea loch which joins Loch Linnhe at Ballachulish ferry.

Following pages: Reflected in the peaceful waters of Loch Awe, between Ben Cruachan and the hills that flank Glen Orchy, Kilchurn Castle belies its warlike past. Kilchurn was a Campbell stronghold and its keep was built by Sir Colin Campbell in 1440, with additions in the sixteenth and seventeenth centuries. In 1746, the year of Culloden, it was occupied by Hanoverian troops at the invitation of the Campbells who were anti-Jacobites. The same gale which blew down the Tay rail bridge in 1879 removed one of Kilchurn's towers, but it remains one of the most splendid and splendidly sited ruins in Scotland.

Right: To many people St. Andrews means one thing: golf. And golf's capital is the Regency style club house of the Royal and Ancient Golf Club which overlooks the first tee and eighteenth green of the Old Course. The Royal and Ancient was founded in 1754 but the game has been played in Scotland at least since 1457 when it was discussed in parliament because it was interfering with the more essential practice of archery. Being a game of the people in Scotland it is not surprising that many courses, including the four full-length ones at St. Andrews, are publicly owned and everyone is entitled to play them, though there is a daily ballot for starting times on the Old Course. This course, one of the most testing in Britain, is often the venue of the British Open Golf Championship and reputations have been made and lost at its notorious 'Road Hole', the seventeenth, where a shade too much 'steam' behind an approach shot can send the ball over the green on to a tarmac roadway from which a return chip requires delicate judgement.

Below: Pittenweem is one of several interesting and highly attractive small ports along a stretch of the Fife coast known as East Neuk. Though it is still an active fishing port, several of the buildings around the harbour have been converted into seaside homes or into antique shops.

region, cut off from the mainstream of north-south tourist traffic. It is now firmly on the tourist route, especially for the growing army who follow golf and come to St. Andrews to worship at the shrine. But there are other attractions: beautiful sands at St. Andrews itself; a fascinating coast from Crail almost to Kirkcaldy – a chain of fishing ports looking over the Firth of Forth to North Berwick and the Bass Rock; Loch Leven beside the Lomond Hills, renowned for its trout and historically famous for the ruined castle on Castle Island. It was from here in 1568 that Mary Queen of Scots, with the help of Willy Douglas, made her dramatic escape to what she hoped would be freedom, but which turned out to be nearly 20 years of detention and ultimate execution at the hands of Elizabeth.

Westward from Perth the road leads through Callander to the Trossachs and Argyll. Some will know that the town of Callander 'acted' the part of Tannochbrae in the English television series 'Dr. Finlay's Casebook'. Visiting addicts will want to pin-point 'Arden House', the home of Finlay, Cameron and Janet. It is called 'Auchengower' and is to the east of the town near the golf course. Argyll is Campbell country

– a name that was for generations associated with the memory of the treachery at Glencoe. The clan headquarters is Inveraray near the head of Loch Fyne, the handsomest small town in Scotland, an eighteenth century creation modernized with impeccable good taste. It is the centre of a romantic countryside with Oban, to the north, the county's second largest town and, in addition, a very popular and attractive holiday centre.

From Oban's harbour MacBrayne's steamer services spread their tentacles over the western isles – except for Seil. Seil is an enchanting little island off the coast south of Oban which can be reached by road. It is joined to the mainland by one of Thomas Telford's bridges, known as 'the bridge over the Atlantic'. So tortuous is the coast of Argyll with deep sea lochs and a multitude of islands that, straightened out, it is estimated it would stretch for 3000 miles (about 5000 km.). Between the lochs, hillsides are covered with endless miles of heather and burns leap from rocky outcrops to tumble through the tree-filled glens. To the far south-west the Mull of Kintyre stretches its long arm towards Northern Ireland and shelters Arran from Atlantic storms.

Below: Culross, a small town on the north shore of the Firth of Forth, is one of the best examples of what a sixteenth century Scottish township must have looked like. The National Trust for Scotland has restored many of its beautiful, interesting and unique sixteenth and seventeenth century buildings including Culross Palace. Even the Electricity Board's sub-station has been hidden in an old house to preserve the overall appearance of the town.

THE LOWLANDS AND BORDER COUNTRY

DESPITE THE RICHNESS and variety of her landscapes, mountains, lochs and moorlands, the extent of her forests, lonely coasts and islands, the diversity of her wildlife and the productivity of her land and seas, Scotland is an industrial country. Wisely – or fortuitously – she concentrates her industry into a central belt roughly between Glasgow and Edinburgh but with a few industrial towns, such as Perth and Dundee, straying from the enclosure. But even within this industrial area there are places of beauty and interest. To its north, Stirling, known as the 'Gateway to the Highlands', has, like Edinburgh, a formidable castle on a volcanic crag towering strategically over the Forth. It was in Stirling Castle that the infant Mary was crowned Queen of Scots soon after her world-weary father, James V, had turned his face to the wall and died in Falkland Palace. A few miles from Stirling, Doune is one of the best preserved

medieval castles in Scotland. Glasgow itself should not be ignored. Its civic architecture is beginning to assume new importance with the revival of respect for the better buildings of the Victorian era, and the City Art Gallery and Museum has the finest collection in Britain outside London.

Edinburgh is a special case: a centre of industry but one where industry plays a secondary role in a city that is in every sense a capital – in its position, in its planning, in its architecture and in the pageant of historical

Below: Rising in the Cheviots, the hills that mark the border country between England and Scotland and the scene of so much bloodshed in the past, Kale Water makes its sparkling way north. Along with many similar streams it flows across Cheviot pastures polka-dotted with sheep to join the salmon-rich Tweed.

events which have shaped its character.

To the east and south of Edinburgh the Great North Road sweeps up from England, crossing the border just north of Berwick-upon-Tweed and skirting the Lammermuir Hills whose heather-glowing slopes give the visitor from the south his first sight of authentic Scotland. At Dunbar, in whose castle Mary stayed with Darnley after Rizzio's murder and later with Bothwell after Darnley's murder, the road swerves west through lovely East Linton and Haddington on its way into the heart of Edinburgh. Haddington is a distinguished town with an architectural legacy that has been faithfully preserved. Nearby is Lennoxlove, originally the home of Maitland of Lethington, Mary Queen of Scots' secretary of state, and now owned by the Duke of Hamilton. There are many relics of the Queen in the house including her death mask.

Above: Traquair House, though enlarged in the reign of Charles I, dates back to the tenth century and is said to be the oldest inhabited house in Scotland. Situated near Peebles, it is open to the public and has several relics of Mary Queen of Scots who stayed there in 1566. A tradition, long since discarded, was that the gates, closed after the Jacobite rising in 1745, would only be re-opened when another Stuart sat on the throne.

Left: On rising ground beside the town loch, Linlithgow Palace, the birth-place of Mary Queen of Scots, still wears an air of majesty in spite of its ruined, fire-stained stones. It was the favourite palace of the Stuarts and although accidentally destroyed by fire in 1746, the charm of its interior is still evident while the views from many of its windows must be virtually unchanged. Linlithgow Loch today does double duty as a sailing lake and a bird sanctuary.

Right: The visitor to Edinburgh can be left in no doubt that he is in an important place for its centre has all the drama and panache of a capital city. And if he happens to be staying near the main railway station, he need only look out from his bedroom window to see almost exactly what this photograph shows. There, serrating the skyline with its towers and battlements, is the castle whose jumbled buildings have been clinging to this volcanic ledge 300 feet (91.4 m.) above the city for nearly 1000 years. The castle's oldest building is the beautifully simple little chapel built in 1076 by Margaret, Malcolm III's queen, later canonized as St. Margaret. It marks the highest point on the rock.

The castle also marks the upper end of the Royal Mile, a line of streets passing the High Kirk of St. Giles, continuing through Canongate down to the Palace of Holyroodhouse, the official residence of the Sovereign in Scotland. This palace, unexpectedly small, is dominated by the green flanks of Arthur's Seat, an extinct 822-foot (250-m.) volcano that serves as a magnificent municipal grandstand from which to view the whole of the city and much of the Firth of Forth and the Pentland Hills. One feature of this panorama which this photograph cannot show (having been taken from its summit) is the 200-foot (61-m.)-high neo-Gothic memorial erected in 1846 to the memory of Scotland's greatest novelist, Sir Walter Scott. Beyond the Scott Monument is the green heart of 'Auld Reekie' (a Scottish term of endearment for the city), Princes Street Gardens, divided into East and West by the Royal Scottish Academy and the National Gallery of Scotland, two impressive buildings which nourish and preserve both Scotland's native art and its rich collection of European masterpieces. On the right of the picture, Princes Street, the main shopping thoroughfare, leads the eye towards the spires of St. Mary's, the cathedral of the Episcopal Church. Behind Princes Street lies the unique 'New Town', instigated in 1770 by Lord Provost Drummond and imaginatively planned by a 23-year-old architect named James Craig. It is a handsome district of wide streets, generous squares and Georgian houses and an outstanding example of intelligent town planning.

For visitors and for most of its inhabitants the highlight of Edinburgh's year is the annual Festival of Arts from the end of August to mid-September when the city throws off any northerly inhibitions it may still possess, flies its flags, lengthens its licensing hours and fills its streets with marching pipers (as shown far right). All in all it's a lovely city.

Below: Kirkcudbright, a picturesque small port at the mouth of the Dee, is the adopted home of a vigorous colony of potters, painters, sculptors and weavers. The vigour seems to have been traditional in the town for a stone in the graveyard records the death of Billy Marshall, a tinker, at the age of 120. According to Sir Walter Scott, Marshall fathered four children after his hundredth birthday. Kirkcudbright is in the centre of an area of Scotland known as Galloway, a region too little visited and of great beauty and peacefulness.

On the coast, the principal holiday town is North Berwick which was 'made' in the latter part of the nineteenth century by the rich and famous who chose it as their exclusive holiday resort. On North Berwick's celebrated golf course cabinet ministers, bankers and millionaires walked farther in a few hours than they would normally walk in a year. From North Berwick Law, a volcanic view-point 613 feet (186 m.) above the town, there is a majestic panorama of the Firth of Forth and the Bass

Rock. Golf courses elbow each other so closely along the southern shores of the Firth of Forth that this stretch is known as the 'Holy Land of Golf'. The championship course at Muirfield is the home of the Ancient and Honourable Company of Edinburgh Golfers who migrated here from Musselburgh in 1891, but the game has been played in Edinburgh since 1457.

To the south and west of Edinburgh, over the green Pentland and Moorfoot Hills, lies a little-known, sparsely-inhabited region of bare

hills and few roads leading to the border country of the Cheviots in the east and to the lovely land of Galloway in the west. By English standards this is mountainous country with hills rising to more than 2000 feet (610 m.), but none has the inhospitable cragginess of the Highlands. Though you may drive for ten miles (16 km.) without seeing a sign of human life, this is a friendly landscape threaded with burns and patterned with clusters of silver birch. Near Moffat, one of Robert Burns' favourite haunts,

both the Clyde and the Tweed rise within a few miles of each other. Leadhills, in the Lowther Hills and one of the highest villages in Scotland, is becoming a popular ski centre.

From the hills that penetrate into the Galloway peninsula which stretches from Dumfries round to Ayr, the rivers Nith, Dee, Cree and Stinchar flow through the rich farming valleys to the Solway Firth and the Irish Sea. This is, to the tourist, a little known and much underrated part of Scotland. Typical of the Solway Firth coast

Further along the coast at Ardrossan, the steamers cross to Arran, an island that has, it is claimed, everything Scotland has to offer in miniature.

Arran's northern 'highlands', with half a dozen peaks rising to more than 2,000 feet (610 metres), are divided from the southern 'lowlands' by The String, an historic mountain road that crosses the island from Brodick to Blackwaterfoot. St. Columba is said to have used this road on his journey from Ireland to Iona.

is the little village of Rockliffe right on the water's edge with Rough Island, a National Trust bird sanctuary, just offshore and accessible on foot at low tide. A little way up the Urr Water estuary is Kippford, a still unspoilt yachting centre. Between the two is the Mote of Mark, a vitrified fort site dating from the sixth century. Important archaeological finds here include iron implements and clay moulds for bronze casting. Across the estuary woodland paths lead to silent, virgin beaches where eighteenth century smugglers landed wines and tobacco when the moon was low.

Up the coast towards Ayr there is another golfer's mecca at Turnberry where the long, red-roofed Turnberry Hotel looks down from its hillside on one of the most testing championship courses in Scotland. Close by is Culzean (pronounced Culain) the splendid cliff-top castle built by Robert Adam for the Earl of Cassillis in 1780. A flat in the castle was given to General Eisenhower as a Scottish home. Now that the castle has been given to the National Trust, the apartment is on view together with many wartime relics of the late President.

Above: In the Firth of Clyde, 15 miles (24 km.) off Ardrossan, lies the 'Scotland-in-miniature' island of Arran. On its east side Lamlash Bay, sheltered by off-shore Holy Island (from where this photograph was taken) was once an anchorage for the biggest ships of the Royal Navy. The island's north end is mountainous and its highest peak, Goat Fell (2866 feet/872 m.) can be plainly seen on the skyline. On a clear day from the summit it is possible to see Scotland, England, Ireland, the Isle of Man and the Outer Hebrides.

NORTHUMBRIA AND
❦ YORKSHIRE ❦

Left: Writing at the end of the seventh century, the Venerable Bede surmised that Hadrian's Wall was built as a defence line against the raiding tribes from the north. Later research has shown that the emperor Hadrian intended it to mark the northern frontier of the Roman Empire in Britain and to be a base from which to attack. In some areas it is still surprisingly complete though in other parts many a farmhouse and barn has benefited from its Roman-hewn stone. It stretches from Wallsend, east of Newcastle upon Tyne, to Bowness, west of Carlisle – a distance of 80 Roman miles or 72 English miles (116 km.).

Right: The bleak winter weather of the high Yorkshire dales is shiveringly captured in this picture of Wensleydale below the Pennine fells with the solitary farmhouse the only sign of life in the frozen landscape. The fells are divided and sub-divided by dry-stone walls. Hundreds of miles of them were built in the eighteenth century when stone was plentiful and labour was cheap. Wensleydale, down which the river Ure flows to join the Ouse between Ripon and York, has given its name to a local, white, crumbly, mild-flavoured cheese originally, but no longer, made from ewe's milk. The main road from Northallerton over the Pennines to Kendal runs up Wensleydale and the Pennine Way crosses it at Hawes.

BETWEEN THE TWO RIVERS Humber and Tweed and between the crests of the Pennines and the North Sea coast lies one of England's most characterful regions. At the northern end is the ancient Saxon kingdom of Northumbria ruled over in times when myth and history were inextricably mixed by such colourfully named kings as Edwin, Ecgfried and Oswald. These Anglo–Saxon monarchs took over when the Romans left Britain and, having subdued the resident tribes, spent much of their time warring with their fellow kings in Mercia or Wessex and with the Picts who came marauding from time to time out of what is now known as Scotland.

King Oswald turned out to be rather different from his fellows. Once pacification was well in hand he decided that it was time these rough, unruly northerners should become Christians like himself. So he asked the influential monastery founded by St. Colomba on Iona to send a missionary to work in Northumbria. They sent a monk called Aidan whose first action was to establish his own island monastery on Lindisfarne – 'the island of the Lincoln people' – off the Northumbrian coast.

The seeds of Christianity which Aidan – later St. Aidan – sowed in Northumbria germinated and spread, eventually reaching far enough south to merge with the mission begun in Canterbury by St. Augustine. From these two points – Lindisfarne, now known as Holy Island, and Canterbury – the conversion of England can

Left : Two miles (3.2 km.) north-west of Helmsley, on the edge of the north Yorkshire moors, a wide grass hillside terrace, belonging to the National Trust, gives this magnificent tree-framed view of Rievaulx Abbey, the earliest large Cistercian church building in England. It was founded in 1131 by members of the Cistercian order who came over from Clairvaux in France. The choir of the abbey church, which many consider to be its finest feature, was added between 1225 and 1230. Both in its architecture and its setting Rievaulx is certainly one of the most imposing ruins to be seen in the north of England.

Above right : Secure on its hill amid the shifting sands of the Northumberland coast, Bamburgh Castle defies the North Sea that thunders at its feet in winter storms. Once the palace of the Anglo-Saxon kings of Northumbria, Bamburgh has often been used as a dramatically regal background in historical films. It was in 1838 that a real-life drama took place here when Grace Darling and her father, the lighthouse-keeper, rowed out into the North Sea in a howling gale to rescue five survivors from the wrecked steamship *Forfarshire*. Bamburgh has commemorated the heroic event with a Grace Darling museum.

Below right : On a pinnacle of rock 70 feet (21.3 m.) high, rising vertically out of an almost circular loop of the river Wear, Durham Cathedral provides the supreme example of the church militant. In the year 687 St. Cuthbert of Lindisfarne Island made the monks at his death-bed promise that if they ever had to leave their island they would take his body with them. Viking raids more than a century later forced them to leave and ultimately they settled at Durham and built a church to house the dead saint's coffin. This church was pulled down by the Normans who built the present muscular cathedral between 1093 and 1133. St. Cuthbert's tomb is behind the high altar and relics of the saint, taken from his coffin in 1827, may be seen in the cathedral library.

Below, far right : Staithes, a red-roofed, white-washed jumble of houses clinging to crumbling clay cliffs above the harbour wall, is one of the many once-important but now declining fishing ports along the Yorkshire coast. Two miles to the west of the village is the highest cliff-top in England – Boulby Cliff, 660 feet (201 m.) high.

be said to have sprung. Today the whole area bristles with reminders that for many centuries Christianity and violence existed side by side. But, in spite of the menacing castles and the defensive solidity of Hadrian's Wall, an air of sanctity pervades the scene: the influence of holy men outweighs the clash of arms. Many people feel this influence most strongly on Holy Island, not so much in the ruins of its monastic buildings where St. Aidan's statue stands as in the glimpse towards the mainland of the little, lonely island, marked with a plain wooden cross, where he is said to have found the solitude he needed for prayer.

The conflicts of this age are epitomized in Durham Cathedral where St. Cuthbert, who

succeeded St. Aidan at Lindisfarne, is buried. On its rocky promontory, virtually surrounded by the river Wear, built even more solidly than the castle which shares its eyrie, Durham Cathedral proclaims the strength of the temporal and ecclesiastical powers which its prince-bishops used to wield.

The air of sanctity is strong in St. Paul's church, Jarrow, where the Venerable Bede, author of England's earliest written history, lived and worked for 50 years up to his death in 753 A.D. Here you can see his high-backed chair looking as though he might have been sitting in it only yesterday and would be again tomorrow. It was the Venerable Bede who first described Hadrian's Wall, then more than 600 years old,

though it is said that he misinterpreted its age and purpose. The wall's construction was ordered by the Emperor Hadrian in about 122 A.D. to mark the most northerly point of the Roman empire. It stretches from the Solway Firth eastwards for 72 miles (116 km.) to Wallsend, just east of Newcastle upon Tyne. It is seen at its best near the picturesquely named village of Twice Brewed, just west of House-steads fort.

The southern half of this region is Yorkshire, England's largest county though now segmented for administrative purposes. It is a land of industrious, down-to-earth, 'brass tack' people made prosperous – initially – by the nourishing pastures of the Yorkshire moors which fattened

and sleekened vast flocks of sheep; then by the purity and power of her great rivers which washed the wool and drove the first mechanical looms, and – later – by the wealth of the coal seams that lie beneath her Pennine borders.

The region has inevitably been scarred by the industrial revolution and its aftermaths but the scars are generally very localized and great areas of Northumberland, Durham and York-shire have remained unaltered since history began. Much is being done, especially around Durham, to eradicate unsightly slag-heaps and restore the land to fertility. The dales that run up into the Pennines and the Cheviots and the moors above them provide some of the best walking country in Britain, only to be compared, some Yorkshiremen say, with the walking on the North York moors between the Vale of York and the sea.

On the North Sea coast stretching from Spurn Head to Berwick-upon-Tweed there is mag-nificent cliff scenery and a number of good seaside places that northerners wisely manage to keep largely to themselves, though many from outside the area have discovered the attractions of Filey, Scarborough, Whitby, Redcar and the delectable and unspoilt coast of Northumber-land. It was at Scarborough, incidentally and surprisingly, that the craze for sea bathing began in the mid-nineteenth century. A few years earlier, on the western edge of the region, two sisters, daughters of an eccentric country parson, were writing novels destined to become classics of English literature. Charlotte and Emily Brontë's home, the Parsonage at Haworth, is preserved very much as it was in the days when 'Jane Eyre' and 'Wuthering Heights' were being written, and it is open for all to see.

Left: The Shambles, one of York's many interesting streets, was mentioned in the Domesday Book and demonstrates what the city must have been like in medieval times when each storey overhung the one below until finally neighbours could shake hands across the street. Originally, as the name implies, a district given over to slaughter-houses, later a street of butchers and today a tourist centre of antique shops, boutiques and galleries.

Below: At the north-east corner of York Minster is the Treasurer's House, parts of which date from the reign of Edward I, although the present house is mainly seventeenth and eighteenth century. The office of treasurer, first created by Thomas, Archbishop of York in 1070, was abolished by Henry VIII and the house passed into private ownership until 1930 when the then owner, Frank Green, gave it to the National Trust.

Above: Harewood House, between Leeds and Harrogate, is the home of the Earl of Harewood, the Queen's cousin. It is a magnificent house begun by John Carr, a Yorkshire architect, in 1759 but modified and finished by Robert Adam who put some of his finest work into its interiors. The most beautiful of the ground floor rooms is the Princess Royal's sitting room shown in this picture. The exquisite Chippendale commode cost £86 in 1773.

CUMBRIA, THE LAKES AND LANCASHIRE

W HEN THE PENNINES were squeezed up to form the backbone of northern England the counties to the east (though they did not exist at the time) got a bigger share of moorland and fell than the counties to the west. As if to compensate for this lop-sided territorial division, a featureless area near the Irish Sea coast erupted to create England's only mountainous region, a miniature Switzerland of incomparable beauty – the Lake District.

It is not a large area – Switzerland itself is 25 times larger – and from the 3118-foot (950 m.) peak of Helvellyn, it is possible on a clear day to see it all – and beyond to the hills of Scotland and the Irish Sea. But within the Lake District's 700 square miles (1800 sq. km.) there are some 100 peaks over 2000 feet (600 m.), 15 lakes (Windermere is over 10 miles (16 km.) long) and ten spectacular waterfalls: a concentration of scenic raw materials that would be hard to duplicate anywhere.

For much of the year the Lake District is thronged with tourists and the M6 motorway, which slices through the north-west region from the West Midlands to the Scottish border, brings an ever-growing stream from the south to enjoy its beauty. 200 years ago its virtues were unsung and its peaks and valleys unvisited. Then, at the beginning of the nineteenth century, a young man who was born and brought up near Grasmere appointed himself what today would be known as the area's Public Relations Officer. He wrote a masterly 'Guide to the Lakes' which was published in 1810 under his own name: William Wordsworth. In it he wrote that the whole area was 'capable of satisfying the most intense cravings for the tranquil and the lovely and the perfect to which man, the noblest of her creatures, is subject'. Lofty idealism of this calibre was exactly what the early Victorians needed to inspire their romantic enthusiasm for nature. The rush to Lakeland was begun. Ruskin was pessimistic about the region's future. In a letter to Canon Rawnsley he said: 'It's all of no use. You will soon have a tourist railway up Scafell, and another up Helvellyn, and another up Skiddaw, and then a connecting line all round.' Happily Ruskin's worst fears have not been fulfilled. As in the case of Stratford-upon-Avon and the Midlands, the intense magnetism of the Lakes has diverted attention

Above: Wordsworth's line 'One bare dwelling, one abode, no more' might easily have been written about this isolated Langdale farmhouse which is only a couple of miles across the fells from the poet's cottage at Grasmere where he lived for 15 years. The road up Langdale from Ambleside, passing through Elterwater and Langdale villages, is one of the classic routes of the Lake District tour, culminating in the impressive view of the Langdale Pikes across Blea Tarn. The four main peaks – Pike o' Stickle, Harrison Stickle, Loft Crag and Pavey Ark – are all above 2000 feet (600 m.) but, in their solitude, seem much higher.

Right: This view of Derwentwater emphasizes one of the great charms of the Lake District: the juxtaposition of a gentle, almost domestic, scene against the wild background of the fells. At the edge of the lake near Friar's Crag (Ruskin's favourite viewpoint) there is a memorial plaque to Canon Rawnsley, a former vicar of Keswick, who was a co-founder of the National Trust in 1895. Much of the Lake District is in the Trust's care.

Right: On the western edge of the Pennines in the river Eden valley north of Appleby, the village of Dufton is a welcoming oasis in a world of moorland and high fells. Here, around a generous village green, most of the houses are built from the local red sandstone which gives the surrounding fields their rich, bronze colouring. In the mid-eighteenth century Dufton was an important lead-mining centre and there is a well-worn path to Great Rundale, a steep hillside beyond Dufton Pike, where the old workings may still be seen. Dufton is on the route of the Pennine Way, the 250-mile (400-km.) track, mapped and signposted, which may be walked from Edale in Derbyshire to Kirk Yetholm on the Scottish side of the Cheviots. A clapper bridge of stone slabs carries the Pennine Way over Dufton's Great Rundale Beck.

Above: Lake District connoisseurs are quick to desert some of the more popular lakes during holiday seasons in order to find the peace and solitude that is Lakeland's great virtue. Loweswater is one of the smaller, less accessible but no less lovely lakes on the western fringe of the district, close to Crummock Water from which it is separated by Loweswater village. This view across the lake from the road through Crabtree shows Holme Wood dominated by the 1781-foot (542-m.) peak of Carling Knott on Loweswater Fell. The circuit of Loweswater, using the road on the north side and lanes and footpaths through Holme Wood on the south, makes a very pleasant hour's walk. Some of the best views of Crummock Water and Buttermere are seen from the shores of Loweswater and the surrounding fells.

Right: The circular drive round Derwentwater (about 12 miles/19 km.) requires the motorist to cross this beautiful stone bridge over the river Derwent at Grange, a small village a mile south of the lake in Borrowdale. The Derwent rises on Scafell Pike and Great Gable above the Borrowdale fells behind Rosthwaite and, in times of heavy rainfall, it cascades down the valley, flooding the lower-lying land and turning Derwentwater and Bassenthwaite Lake into one vast stretch of water. A mile above the bridge, at the side of the road, is the Bowder Stone, a rock estimated to weigh 2000 tons (2032 tonnes) which has at some time fallen from the surrounding crags. It appears to be finely balanced and the more daring are invited to climb a ladder to the summit to prove the point.

from the rest of the region which is surprisingly interesting and attractive, though not without industrial scars around Liverpool and Manchester, its two principal – and dynamic – cities.

To the north of the region there is another and very different city – Carlisle, the sentinel city near the Scottish border and a one-time fort on Hadrian's Wall which ended some 12 miles (19 km.) to the west. It is the centre of a wild and solitary though fertile region flanked by Pennine moorlands to the east and the racing tidal waters of the Solway Firth to the west. All down this Cumbrian coast, except for the industrialized strip between Maryport and Whitehaven, there are deserted sandy beaches where the only sounds are the drag of retreating waves and the plaintive cry of sea-birds.

For the gregarious there is always Blackpool and Morecambe and the other Lancashire coastal resorts (not forgetting the Isle of Man) where the northerners show the rest of the world how they like to enjoy themselves even if 'Kiss-me-quick' hats are not everyone's idea of a good time. It is easy to be toffee-nosed about Blackpool, but northerners are very demanding people and for the food they like and the entertainment they enjoy the standards they demand are high.

Inland from Blackpool and north towards Lancaster lies one of those stretches of countryside that, to the southerner at any rate, is unexpected in Lancashire: the Forest of Bowland, a green and brown wilderness of high pasture and fell stretching from close to Clitheroe almost to Lancaster. The only road across the Forest

climbs through the Trough of Bowland, a stream-bordered, tree-lined valley sheltering under the steep flank of Blaze Moss, a 1700-foot (518 m.) high hill.

For those blessed with the 'seeing eye' there is much beauty to be found in the harbour bustle of Liverpool, first settled nearly 2000 years ago, firmly established on the West Indian trade and now the largest port in Britain. It is the only city in the country which can claim to have two cathedrals both built in the present century, though it is probably more widely known as the birth-place of the Beatles from whose rocket-like careers the whole 'pop' idiom in Britain seems to have sprung.

Liverpool shares its estuary – the Mersey – with Manchester via the Manchester Ship

Canal which penetrates right into the heart of Trafford Park, the city's main industrial zone. Though 35 miles (56 km.) from the sea the port of Manchester handles more cargo than either Bristol or Glasgow.

The old Lancashire saying 'Where there's muck there's money' is at last beginning to lose its point when one looks at the best of the re-development that is going on in some of the Lancashire towns such as Blackburn, Bolton and Burnley. Smokeless zones have been created and proved surprisingly effective in areas that at one time seemed doomed to exist under growing layers of soot. Manchester alone has 30 square miles (80 sq. km.) of smokeless zones and to anyone re-visiting the city the improvement is dramatic.

Yes, there is plenty to see and do in the north-west outside the Lake District where, as an old Yorkshireman once remarked, 'there's nowt but scenery'.

Left: Five miles (8 km.) south of Kendal (which was saved from extinction by the arrival of the M6 motorway) Levens Hall welcomes visitors during the summer months. It is a fine Elizabethan house and in the unique gardens weird shapes abound and wild animals are tethered by their roots – for Levens Hall has the most noted topiary gardens in the whole of the north of England. Designed by Beaumont, a pupil of Le Notre, at the beginning of the eighteenth century when 'clipping' was all the rage (had someone just invented shears?), Levens Hall gardens have retained much of the original plan but flower beds and borders have been added to give colour to the box, holly, yew and beech ornamental trees.

The house is based on a fourteenth century 'peel-tower', the fortified refuge to which the family would retreat when there was a threatened invasion by the Scots. In the house there are some fine pictures, including one by Rubens, also the Sevres coffee service, originally ordered for Napoleon's mother, which the Duke of Wellington brought back to England as a gift for his niece, Lady Mary Bagot, an ancestor of the present owner of Levens Hall.

Opposite, below: Blackpool's air, they say, is more like Guinness than champagne – a supportable theory when one considers that the exhilarating breezes from the sea must originate near Dublin where the better half of Black Velvet is brewed. Blackpool, whose tower is its trade mark and whose 'Golden Mile' must be the biggest money-spinner since the seaside was invented, is a rollicking, rumbustious resort on the Lancashire coast, very handy for the densely populated and highly industrialized areas of the hinterland. At the beginning of this century a day at the seaside was the most that many families could expect while with today's longer holidays it is easy to understand why Blackpool can expect some eight million visitors during the season – a season that is stretched to October by the 'illuminations' that turn Blackpool's six-mile (9.6 km.) sea-front into a cross between Disneyland and the Aurora Borealis.

Below: In keeping with its maritime significance, Liverpool has allowed some of its most prominent buildings to occupy the waterfront behind its seven miles (11 km.) of docks and its half-mile (800 m.) of floating landing stage (it can rise and fall as much as 30 feet (9 m.) on a good spring tide). Seen in this photograph, taken from Canning Dock, are the new Cunard building, the restored Docks Board building and the indestructible Royal Liver (to rhyme with 'diver') building. Most prominent and most characterful of these three is the famous Liver building, a monumental office block of anonymous architectural style, ten storeys high, with twin towers that allow the 'Liver' birds perched on the domes to survey the Mersey and all the shipping on it from a height of some 250 feet (76 m.) above high water mark. The birds have become Liverpool's emblem but their ancestory is something of a mystery. They are of no known species. One theory is that the Liver bird was a seventeenth century invention to explain the derivation of the city's name but that seems unnecessary for, according to the gazetteer of the 'Reader's Digest' atlas of the British Isles, it means 'pool with thick water'. A more logical explanation is that the twigs they are carrying in their beaks are, on closer examination (and who could do that but a helicopter pilot?) fronds of a species of seaweed called 'lyver'.

The two cathedrals are both of this century; the Anglican, designed by Sir Giles Gilbert Scott and begun in 1904, had to be modified because of escalating costs; the Roman Catholic Metropolitan Cathedral, designed by Sir Frederick Gibberd, was consecrated in 1967. In the Liverpool Philharmonic, the city has one of Britain's front-rank orchestras and, in the Walker Art Gallery, one of the foremost collections of European and English paintings.

THE MIDLANDS

Right: Apart from the addition of some Gothic windows during the last century, very few alterations have been made to Compton Wynyates since it was begun by Edmund Compton in 1480 and finished by his son William. The mellow brick house surrounds a courtyard and is itself surrounded by formal topiary gardens and rising parkland which places the house in a hollow. Indeed, in Elizabethan maps it is marked as 'Compton-in-ye-Hole'. The house was originally moated but the Comptons had to fill in the moat after the Civil War as a penalty for supporting the Royalist cause. Earl Compton, the present occupant, opens the house and gardens in the summer months. It is 10 miles (16 km.) west of Banbury.

THE CENTRAL COUNTIES OF ENGLAND, known as the Midlands, have, as you would expect, a middle or more properly a centre. That distinction is claimed by the village of Meriden in Warwickshire whose medieval cross on the green is said to be the exact geographical centre of England. It is possible to give some substance to this claim by drawing a circle of about 60 miles (96 km.) radius around the cross and finding that its perimeter encloses an area of over 10,000 square miles (26,000 sq. km.) made up of the counties of Cheshire, Derbyshire, Nottinghamshire, Lincolnshire, Leicestershire, Northamptonshire, Bedfordshire, Warwickshire, Gloucestershire, Worcestershire, Herefordshire, Staffordshire and Shropshire. The definition is far from precise: boundaries very rarely are. If, for instance, you say that the Midlands are those parts of England which have no sea coast you are forced to omit Lincolnshire and Cheshire, both of which have. So it is best to stop trying to define the Midlands too precisely and accept the fact that they are diverse, diverting and definitely underrated.

Touristically the Midlands suffer from the widely-held canard that the only good thing they possess is Stratford-upon-Avon and the Shakespeare cult upon which it thrives. Stratford *is* a lovely town, historically, literarily and theatrically important, but to visit it without much more than a glance at the surrounding regions is to neglect much of England's most delectable scenery and ignore some of her richest treasures.

Search as you will, it is difficult to find a common denominator in the Midlands. How can there be in a region whose industries vary from coal mining and heavy engineering to lace making and basket weaving, and whose scenery changes from the muscular gritstone 'edges' of Derbyshire to the errant loops of the Ouse in Bedfordshire? The practical thing to do is to take a random dip into some of the individual Midland counties and stimulate the appetite by sampling. In this way you discover that Warwickshire has more than Shakespeare. It has, for instance, the stately ruins of Kenilworth Castle where Robert Dudley, Earl of Leicester, entertained Elizabeth I so lavishly that he all but bankrupted himself. It also has the massive

Left: The Lord Warwick whom Shakespeare described as the 'proud setter-up and puller-down of kings' held Edward IV prisoner in Warwick Castle in 1469, and his descendants have lived in it ever since. The present occupant is Lord Brooke, the Earl of Warwick's son and heir. Sir Walter Scott, who was something of an authority on castles, thought Warwick was 'the fairest monument of ancient and chivalrous splendour which yet remains uninjured by time'. It is certainly everyone's idea of what a medieval fortress should look like. Below its sheer walls the Avon flows placidly on its way to Stratford. The interior of the castle was transformed into a stately home in the seventeenth century but badly damaged by fire in 1770. In the state apartments, which are open to the public, there is a magnificent collection of furniture and armour. The pictures include works by Velasquez and Rubens.
Above: Louth, a market town serving a wide agricultural area of Lincolnshire, has managed to preserve some of the best features of its Georgian past; its street market being one of them. The 300 foot (91 m.) spire of its sixteenth century church is a familiar landmark in the flat country and is used as a leading mark by shipping entering the Humber.

Below: The Early English nave of Lincoln is built of limestone from the hill on which the cathedral stands, but the piers are ornamented with multiple shafts of Purbeck marble. On the easternmost pier on the north side of the Choir, the famous 'Lincoln Imp' leers down from among intricately carved foliage. This grotesque figure, the work of some jocular medieval mason, went almost unnoticed until the middle of the nineteenth century when James Usher, a local jeweller, designed him into a tie-pin which was presented to the Prince of Wales (later Edward VII) and made a fortune from replicas.

Below: Lincoln Cathedral on Steephill, 250 feet (76 m.) above the lower streets, dominates the city and the surrounding countryside. It was one of the first of the Norman cathedrals and must surely be the only one in England to have been damaged by earthquake, an event which happened in 1185. According to a contemporary account the cathedral was 'cleft from top to bottom'. Rebuilding began almost at once and the cathedral as it stands today was virtually completed by 1280. Since that time the only major alteration has been the heightening of the three towers which are such a feature.

Far left: One of the most beautiful stretches of the river Wye is at Symonds Yat, between Ross-on-Wye and Monmouth, where the river, after passing through a narrow gorge, makes a great five-mile (8-km.) loop round Huntsham Hill, failing to complete its total encirclement by a mere quarter of a mile (400 m.). This view is from Yat Rock on the Gloucestershire side of the river. 'Yat' is an old English word for gate.

Opposite, bottom: To get away from what some people see as the over-exploitation of Shakespeare in the streets of Stratford-upon-Avon, it is only necessary to walk a short distance along the banks of the Avon to get this pastoral view of St. Mary's Church where the poet is buried. For Shakespeare to have a tomb at all seems somewhat surprising for there can be no playwright in the world whose works are still so much alive and still so relevant.

and menacing defences of Warwick Castle looming over the Avon, still inhabited by the Warwick family after 600 years – one of the few medieval castles in England still inhabited.

Neighbouring Northamptonshire, except near the Warwickshire borders, is a flatter, more open landscape, mainly agricultural but industrially important for its deposits of iron ore at Corby. Being a limestone area the county has beautiful churches, many with elegant spires, and castles both inhabited and ruined. One evocative spot is a mere grassy mound beside the river Nene. Here stood Fotheringhay Castle where Mary Queen of Scots was beheaded in 1587 after 19 years of frustrating detention during which she had been shuttled around the Midlands from one

built by the Countess of Shrewsbury (Bess of Hardwick) with the money accumulated from four advantageous marriages; Kedleston Hall, for 800 years the home of the Curzons; and Melbourne Hall which gave its name to Melbourne, Australia and where Thomas Cook, of travel fame, began his working life as a gardener's boy.

In Worcestershire the Malvern Hills rise like a shark's fin above the distant Vale of Evesham, the market garden of the Midlands. It was while wandering on these hills one summer evening that Sir Edward Elgar heard a voice singing the lovely folk-tune which became the theme of his Introduction and Allegro for Strings. Elgar's music captures the essence of Worcestershire

Preceding pages: The Lord Leycester Hospital in Warwick was founded in 1571 by Robert Dudley, Earl of Leicester and favourite of Queen Elizabeth I, as a hospital (in the early sense of the word) for 'poor and impotent' persons. The buildings were originally the headquarters of Warwick's Town Guilds which were dispersed in 1546. Their chapel – St. James – can be seen to the left of the picture. Today the Lord Leycester Hospital carries on the intentions of its founder as a home for retired or disabled ex-servicemen.

Left: Though the canals of Britain are individually small, the system was, in its heyday, very extensive and highly important when railways were non-existent and roads almost unusable. Several of the canals continue to make a small but useful contribution to the carriage of goods and there is a movement to restore them as a cheap and efficient means of transportation. Meanwhile many of them are being restored for recreational use for boating and fishing, and there are several centres where boats may be hired by the week to explore the beautiful stretches of England's canal system. Because of their meagre width a special type of barge known as a 'narrow boat' was developed for British canals. The narrow boat shown here with its musical owner is a working boat at Stoke Bruerne on the Grand Junction canal in Northamptonshire. At Stoke Bruerne the canal disappears into a tunnel to emerge over 3000 yards (2743 m.) away at Blisworth. There is a fascinating Waterways Museum in an old warehouse at Stoke Bruerne illustrating the vital role played by canals in England in the eighteenth century.

Right: Mam Tor, a 1700-foot (518 m.) mountain in north Derbyshire, is the southern outpost of the region known as the High Peak. This is the really rugged northern half of Derbyshire's Peak District, an area of rocky outcrops on high moorlands, crossed by the Pennine Way, the track which conducts determined walkers 250 miles (400 km.) to the Scottish border.

People living in the Midlands and North of England have long regarded the Peak District as their natural playground for walking, climbing, pot-holing (the limestone hills are riddled with subterranean caverns), sailing, fishing or just relaxing. Indeed, it was largely the pressure of public opinion generated by the thousands of walkers from Manchester and Sheffield that led, in the early 1930s, to the public being granted access to the privately owned mountains and moors in the area and to the establishment, in 1951, of the Peak District National Park. This Park – it covers 542 square miles (1400 sq. km.) and includes the whole of north-west Derbyshire as well as parts of the adjoining counties of Staffordshire and Yorkshire – ensures a strict control over development in a region of great natural beauty and high amenity value.

Mam Tor has been known since Elizabethan times as the shivering mountain because of the way its almost continuous landslides of shale and grit reflect the sunlight.

custodian's house to another's. Of special interest particularly to American visitors is Sulgrave Manor which is the home of George Washington's ancestors.

Derbyshire is a complete contrast, at least in the north where the so-called Peak District is to be found. To the question which many people ask: 'Which is *the* Peak?' the answer is simple: there is not one. The district gets its name from the Peacs, an ancient British tribe which lived in the area before the Romans came. In the Peak District National Park, the Pennine Way – a 250-mile (400-km.) track for walkers leading to the Scottish border – begins at Edale beneath the massive 2000-foot (600-m.) hump of Kinder Scout. Derbyshire's stately homes are world-famous: Chatsworth, home of the Duke of Devonshire; Haddon Hall, scene of Dorothy Vernon's romantic elopement; Hardwick Hall,

as well, if not better, than words can ever hope to do.

The most westerly county of the Midlands – Herefordshire – has the river Wye as its signature tune. It rises in the Cambrian mountains, a clean, dancing river, plays its slow movement as it passes the pink stone pile of Hereford Cathedral, swings into a five-mile (8-km.) loop at Symonds Yat and finally separates England from Wales before merging with the Severn below Chepstow.

Shropshire has become inextricably associated with A. E. Housman, the poet who died in 1936. He wrote nostalgically of Wenlock Edge, the Wrekin and the country bordering the upper reaches of the Severn. That Housman was a Worcestershire man is one of those quirks of topography in which the well-mixed Midlands specialize.

❧EAST ANGLIA❧

I N EAST ANGLIA the sky comes into its own: clear, luminous blue arching up from limitless horizons to proclaim that East Anglia has no end and no beginning. And, indeed, in some respects it has not. On its east side the hungry sea gnaws away at its cliffs and dunes while to the west, where huge shallow meres and marshes once cut it off from the rest of England, today's fenland fields – hedgeless acres of rich dark soil – spread endlessly outward towards the sky.

But to set some limits, however arbitrary, East Anglia may be said to cover certainly the counties of Norfolk and Suffolk, possibly parts of Lincolnshire where it borders the Wash and the estuaries of Essex, and finally Cambridgeshire where its ill-defined inland boundaries lie. Physically the area has much in common with the Netherlands, but what all East Anglians share is a sturdy – some call it stubborn – independence bred into them through centuries of isolation from their neighbours.

Until the seventeenth century the Fens were a watery waste stretching from south of the Isle of Ely (which was literally an island then) as far as the Wash, the great shallow indentation of the North Sea separating western Norfolk from

Below: Salt flats and sand dunes like these abound along the coasts of Norfolk and Suffolk and are poor protection against the North Sea. In the floods of January 1952, when many people were drowned, dozens of coastal villages were inundated though their medieval churches, built on rising ground, escaped. The East Anglian coast is gradually retreating and, over the centuries, as at Dunwich, whole towns and villages have been swallowed by the waves.

Right: Sailing for pleasure on the Norfolk Broads became popular only towards the end of the last century. As the work of the trading wherries and the reed cutters declined, the holidaymaker took over and turned these lovely waterways into a playground for amateur sailors. In recent years a sail has become a comparatively rare sight as more and more visitors demand power-driven craft. As a result these waters are becoming a growing menace to the uniquely rich wild life of the area.

Right, inset: Willy Lott's cottage, adjoining Flatford Mill, was the subject of one of John Constable's most famous paintings. So little has the scene changed that Constable would have no difficulty in recognizing the cottage as it is today from this photograph.

eastern Lincolnshire. To strangers to the area the Fens presented an almost impassable barrier and anyone who did manage to find his way across was regarded with suspicion and dubbed a 'foreigner'. Even today in East Anglia you will often hear people born in other parts of England referred to as foreigners.

As early as the reigns of Elizabeth I and James I plans were made to drain the Fens, but it was not until Charles I was insecurely on the throne that any practical steps were taken. A Dutch engineer named Vermuyden was engaged to master-mind the operation but Charles ran out of money. Then came the Civil War and

operations were again delayed. Finally in 1653, the original plan was completed and hundreds of square miles of land were gradually brought under the plough.

Today on the Isle of Ely stands – and has stood for nearly 1000 years – one of England's architectural treasures: Ely Cathedral, begun in 1083 on the site of an earlier Benedictine abbey. In 1322 the Norman central tower collapsed to be replaced by something quite unique in ecclesiastical architecture: the 'Octagon', a gigantic eight-sided lantern tower 74 feet (22.5 m.) across. In the flat lands of the fens it stands on its low island like a lighthouse on a hill. South

of Ely lies the city and university of Cambridge with some half-dozen of its world-famous colleges backing on to the river. The 'backs' as they are called, particularly in a daffodil-rich spring, are one of the great visual experiences of East Anglia – a perfect blend of young growth and ancient architecture bordering the placid waters of the Cam.

Eastward from the Fens the land rises markedly, though the naming by some atlases of the low hills of Suffolk as the 'East Anglian Heights' rather overstates the case. All the same East Anglia is not as flat as it is often said to be. Both Norfolk and Suffolk are endowed with

gentle hills and valleys which give much of the landscape a pleasant, undulating intimacy beneath the generous skies. 'You can, in no direction, go a quarter of a mile', wrote William Cobbett in his 'Rural Rides', 'without finding views that a painter might crave'. And, indeed, anyone familiar with the works of John Crome, John Sell Cotman, John Constable and Thomas Gainsborough – East Anglians to a man – will know exactly what he meant, for these artists captured the simple charm of East Anglia in what are now considered to be the finest English landscape paintings of the early nineteenth century.

Left: The East Anglian wool trade which, in the fourteenth and fifteenth centuries, made this region one of the wealthiest in England, has bequeathed some dazzling architectural gems. One of its richest jewel boxes is the Suffolk village of Lavenham. In the village centre, whichever way you turn, there are beautifully preserved (though internally modernized) medieval houses. It is easy to see that the Lavenham Preservation Committee has been busy in the village, but so have others. Trust House Hotels, who own 'The Swan', took over the Wool Hall, which was at one time threatened with demolition, and have incorporated it into the hotel. The Guildhall in Market Square is in the care of the National Trust to whom it was given in 1951 by Sir Cuthbert Quilter and the Lavenham Preservation Committee. A small local museum is housed on the first floor, and the Guildhall, some adjoining cottages and the Old Chapel are used as a community centre.

Above: Though modernity has crept perilously close, Elm Hill remains a sensitively preserved corner of medieval Norwich, winding from Prince's Street to Wensum Street and all within the shadow of Norwich's Norman cathedral. Elm Hill is a cobbled, traffic-free street which broadens out at one point into a square courtyard where stands the elm tree which gives the street its name. At each end of the street is a church – SS. Simon and Jude and St. Peter's, Hungate – neither of which is used for services. St. Peter's is a beautiful, small, fifteenth century church built by Margaret Paston (of the Paston Letters family) which now serves as a museum of ecclesiastical art. The date 1460 appears on a buttress of the porch. The houses on Elm Hill are a harmonious mixture of medieval timber and plaster buildings sandwiched between Georgian façades. The juxtaposition is utterly successful. Elm Hill recently won an international street lighting award.

Left: It is not a coincidence that there is a strong similarity between Ely and Winchester cathedrals. Abbot Simeon, who was responsible for the planning of Ely, was the brother of Bishop Walkelin who was building his cathedral in Winchester at the same time. When Simeon died 12 years later (he was 87 when he took on the job!) Ely had barely progressed beyond the foundation stage. Abbot Richard, who succeeded Simeon, continued to build to the original plan and by 1106 the choir was completed and the bodies of four saints – Etheldreda, Sexburga, Withburga and Ermenhilda – were moved from the old Saxon church and reinterred behind the high altar.

By 1189 Simeon's original plan had taken shape with the completion of the massive west tower, much as it is today. The Lady Chapel, placed unusually to the north of the choir, was begun in 1321. Though still a beautiful chapel, it has lost much of its original magnificence. Its windows were ablaze with stained glass and every arcade and niche was richly decorated with scenes from the legendary life of the Virgin. The glass was stolen and the carvings mutilated by reforming iconoclasts during the Reformation.

A year after the lady chapel was begun the cathedral suffered a major disaster when the Norman central tower collapsed bringing down the adjoining bays of the choir with it. But out of disaster came triumph when Alan de Walsingham built over the central crossing a stone octagon, settling above it a wooden lantern sheathed in lead and framed with eight enormous angle-posts cut from oak trees more than 60 feet (18 m.) high. Ely's lantern (shown above) is unique – one of the wonders of medieval engineering and carpentry and, architecturally, a masterpiece.

Above: King's College Chapel, seen beyond the punters on the Cam, is not only the architectural gem of Cambridge but also England's finest example of the Perpendicular style. It was begun by Henry VI in 1446 but, because of delays caused by the Wars of the Roses, not completed until 1515, six years after Henry VIII's accession. The next 26 years were occupied by the Flemish glaziers putting in the superb windows. In 1962 the chapel received a splendid gift: 'The Adoration of the Magi' by Paul Rubens. It is now the chapel's altarpiece. In this picture, King's College is to the right of the chapel and the beautifully proportioned Clare College, built in 1638, to the left.

Below: This butcher's shop in Newmarket, heartland of the 'sport of kings' since the seventeenth century, exudes an almost Regency swagger with the Royal Arms proudly displayed. Their presence indicates that the proprietor of the shop has been granted the Royal Warrant by the Queen, the Duke of Edinburgh or the Queen Mother to supply goods to the Royal household concerned. It is a Royal favour not lightly granted. The proprietor – or in the case of a company, one of its directors – is personally responsible for seeing that the nearly 40 rules to be observed by holders of the Royal Warrant, drawn up by the Lord Chamberlain's office, are properly observed.

In spite of the splendours of Cambridge, the industrial growth of Ipswich and the antiquities of Colchester, Norwich is really the queen of East Anglian cities though its position today bears no comparison with its status in the Middle Ages when, after London and Bristol, it was the third city in the kingdom, its prosperity based on wool. In Norwich everything combines to convey this former prominence and a continuing prosperity coupled with an evident civic pride. This prosperity, in which the whole of East Anglia shared, resulted in the building of some splendid houses and – for today's needs – an over-supply of churches; inner Norwich alone has 32.

The decline of the wool trade coincided with the rise of agriculture in East Anglia and to two of Norfolk's large landowners – Townshend of Raynham and Coke of Holkham – must go the credit for laying in the eighteenth century the foundations of much modern agricultural practice, enabling the region's widespread sandy soils to produce heavy crops of grain and sugar beet. East Anglia has a long and fascinating sea coast with stretches of sands interspersed with marshland noted for the richness and variety of its bird and plant life. The Norfolk Broads have become a rather over-popular playground in recent years and further south the estuaries of Suffolk and Essex are also centres of great sailing activity.

One of the charms of East Anglia lies in the fact that it is a region that is only lightly industrialized and it is evident that where the pressures of working are less, the rewards of living certainly do seem, by contrast, to be incomparably richer.

✥ LONDON ✥

OF ALL THE WORLD'S great capital cities, London appears to be the most magnetic, for statistics show that of every 100 people who come to Britain more than 90 of them visit London. Their reasons for doing so cannot be quite so crisply expressed. The British Tourist Authority asks visitors why they come and the most recent survey showed that the main attraction of London was its 'history and tradition'. The next reason for coming was given as the umbrella answer – 'everything'. The city that has everything probably best sums up London's appeal. But in addition London, in recent years, has developed – and this is impossible to quantify – an informality about its daily life which seems to suit the present generation of tourists.

London's road traffic is certainly informal but this is due to a great extent to the unplanned nature of the city or, to be precise, cities. For London is a tale of two cities, one beginning as a Roman settlement and forming the basis of what is known today as the City of London, the other, about two miles (3 km.) to the west, growing up

around the abbey which Edward the Confessor founded in 1050 (though scholars believe there was an earlier abbey on the site).

The City of London, filled to capacity by workers during the day, relatively unoccupied at night, is bounded by the Thames to the south and covers rather more than 330 acres (133 hectares) which the Romans enclosed within their defensive wall. When William the Conqueror arrived in 1066 he found huge gaps in the Roman wall where the Londoners of Anglo-Saxon times had helped themselves to useful blocks of Kentish ragstone and Roman bricks, so he plugged one gap with the White Tower which is part of the present Tower of London and the earliest surviving building in the City.

While the City busied itself with commerce, Westminster, the city around the Abbey, became the centre of government. Westminster Hall, adjacent to the present Houses of Parliament and built by William Rufus, is the only remaining building of the Palace of Westminster to which the kings of England moved from Winchester. Here King Charles I was sentenced to death in

Left: On the second Saturday in June the Queen rides out from Buckingham Palace to take part in the Trooping the Colour ceremony on Horse Guards Parade. The parade marks her 'official' birthday (her true birthday is 21st April).

1649. Although Westminster retains its boundaries the city has, in effect, grown to absorb all of what is known as the West End where most of 'visitors' London' is to be found.

Though both these cities have grown and prospered and have lived together for close on 1000 years they have never made up their minds to become legally married. The City of London maintains its independence in many ways. For instance, before the Queen may enter the City

she must stop at Temple Bar and ask permission of the Lord Mayor of London who, symbolically, surrenders the Sword of State to her. It is only a formality but it emphasizes the City's status.

Outer London – the suburbs which the visitor rarely sees – are former villages which have been absorbed into the body of the great spreading monster. Some, like Dulwich and Hampstead, have preserved their individuality, many are amorphous. But beyond the suburbs, though now officially in London, places like Richmond and Hampton Court, Kew Gardens and Syon House are high on the tourist list and well worth the journey.

London has no master plan, no dramatic *mise en scène*. Its charm lies in its irregularities; in the placing of important buildings in unimportant places. There are, of course, exceptions: the Mall from Admiralty Arch up to Buckingham Palace has a regal air, particularly on some state occasion when banners flank the tree-lined route. Trafalgar Square could be distinctly grand were it not for some very drab buildings on two of its sides. The view of the Houses of Parliament from the terrace of the Festival Hall is a heart-lifting sight, but here again the plebeian girders of Hungerford Bridge mar the foreground.

Another unexpected feature of London is the number, variety and beauty of its parks and open spaces. St. James's Park was laid out by John Nash as a front garden for Buckingham Palace,

Above: The magnificent interior of the House of Lords debating chamber was designed by Augustus Pugin who loved Gothic detail and rich reds and browns. The centre-piece is the throne from which the Queen speaks when opening Parliament. In the niches above the throne and between the windows are statues of the 18 barons who persuaded King John to sign Magna Carta in 1215.

but it is open for all to enjoy and the view from the bridge over the lake might be of some oriental city shimmering in the limpid sunlight. Hyde Park is less of a private garden and more of an open space but trees and the Serpentine judiciously break the flatness and, in the adjoining Kensington Gardens, there are some unfrequented corners where the quack of ducks and the scuttering of blackbirds in the undergrowth are the only sounds to be heard.

What overseas visitors marvel at most – and what most Londoners take for granted – is the incredible collection of art treasures and historical objects to be found in the city. To list all

the famous art galleries and museums would be tedious and unhelpful but to say that London collectively has the richest concentration of art objects of any city in the world – and that includes Paris and Rome – is no exaggeration.

More than most cities, London has been shaped and given character by the men and women who have been its citizens. The blue plaques on the fronts of many houses record where they lived or worked. One of them at 17, Gough Court, off Fleet Street, marks the home of Dr. Johnson who said: 'When a man is tired of London he is tired of life; for there is in London all that life can afford.'

Preceding pages: The Houses of Parliament make a fairy-tale-castle silhouette across the Thames. Designed by Charles Barry and Augustus Pugin, they were built between 1840 and 1860 to replace those destroyed in a disastrous fire in 1834. The Victoria Tower is on the left, the Clock Tower (popularly known as Big Ben) is on the right. *Below:* In their ceremonial red and gold uniforms the Yeoman Warders are easily confused with the Yeoman of the Guard, the Queen's bodyguard known as 'Beefeaters'. The Yeoman Warders are the guardians and guides at the Tower of London. *Right:* This nineteenth-century-Gothic building is the Royal Courts of Justice. Opposite its main

entrance a 'griffin' statue marks Temple Bar, the end of Westminster and the beginning of the City of London.

Bottom right : Sir Christopher Wren's St. Paul's Cathedral was begun nine years after its predecessor had been destroyed in the Fire of London (1666). Wren's tomb in the crypt bears the famous inscription: 'Reader, if you would seek his monument, look around you'.

Below: The view from the elegant little bridge over the lake in St. James's Park is one of the most beautiful and unexpected in London. Across the shimmering water the great blocks of government offices in Whitehall take on an almost oriental opulence while, in the opposite direction, Buckingham Palace appears to float majestically 'all bright and glittering in the smokeless air'. There is a large and varied collection of waterfowl living in and around the lake. At the Whitehall end the pelicans have an island all to themselves. The Mall, the ceremonial route leading from Buckingham Palace, runs along the north side of the park.

Left: Hampstead is one of the few London suburbs that has managed to preserve its particular character and individuality. When medicinal waters were discovered here in the eighteenth century, an obscure out-of-town village quickly grew into a fashionable spa.

Holly Hill, shown in the photograph, is one of the several steep, tree-lined streets of elegant Georgian houses leading off the busy High Street. Near here, at Grove Lodge, was the home of John Galsworthy, author of the 'Forsyte Saga'. Romney and Keats also lived nearby. Hampstead Heath, nearly 800 acres (300 hectares) of open country four miles (6 km.) from the heart of London, adjoins Hampstead and is one of London's favourite open spaces. John Constable, who lived in Hampstead for several years before his death in 1837 (he is buried in the churchyard of St. John's, Church Row) did a famous painting of Hampstead Heath which may be seen in the Tate Gallery.

Top: Regent Street was originally constructed by John Nash in the years between 1813 and 1823 to connect the Prince Regent's two houses, one in Regent's Park and the other in the Mall. All that remains of Nash's design is the curve which sweeps into Piccadilly Circus; the façades were rebuilt in the 1920s. Regent Street is one of London's main shopping streets, housing such familiar stores as Swan and Edgar, Austin Reed, Aquascutum, Libertys, Hamleys and Dickens and Jones.

Above: The London policeman, or 'Bobby' as he is called (after Sir Robert Peel who reorganized the London police force in 1829), is the visitor's friendliest source of information about the capital. Whether it is finding the way, catching a bus, seeking advice or merely asking the time, the chances are that the London policeman knows the answer, or he can tell where to find it. There are approximately 21,000 police in Greater London. Unlike many police abroad the London policeman is unarmed.

THE THAMES VALLEY
AND COTSWOLDS

Left: Before the Second World War, the 'Cliveden Set', as the guests at the Astors' political weekends were known, enjoyed this glimpse of the Thames from the top of the beech-clad hill on which Cliveden stands. The big tree is known as the Canning Oak as it was a favourite viewpoint for George Canning, British foreign minister and, briefly, prime minister at the beginning of the nineteenth century. Today Cliveden belongs to the National Trust and everyone can enjoy the house and gardens.

Right: Chipping Camden is the most northerly town of the Cotswolds, a line of hills in Gloucestershire and Oxfordshire and one of Britain's favourite and most picturesque tourist areas. Typical of the Cotswolds, Chipping Camden is largely built of the distinctive honey-coloured oolitic freestone which is relatively soft but surprisingly durable. William Grevel's House in the High Street is almost 600 years old and nearly every building in the town centre is pre-1800. The handsome fifteenth century church contains early brasses and monuments to the wealthy wool merchants who built it, and the Jacobean Market Hall must be one of the most photographed buildings in England.

THE THAMES is a wealthy river deriving its substantial income from a long list of benefactors: the Rodings of Essex and the Downs of Dunstable; the Chilterns and the Vale of Aylesbury, the Uplands of Northamptonshire and the Vale of White Horse; the Downs of Marlborough and Lambourn and the Cotswold Hills; the Heights of Hindhead and Haslemere and the suburban slopes of the North Downs. From all these surrounding hills and valleys tributaries trickle, gurgle, flow and surge towards the Thames to make it the longest, largest and most picturesque river in England. And what a fascinating collection of names these tributaries have: Cherwell, Windrush, Stort, Ock, Roding, Evenlode, Loddon, Kennet, Mole, Wey and a dozen others. Each has a character of its own; each adds its individuality to the complex character of 'sweet Thames'.

The Thames in London is a tidal river, rising and falling some 20 feet (6 m.) with each tide, but above Teddington (Tide-ending-town) it changes its life style, throws off its sober, workaday suit and becomes a cheerful, beflagged pleasure-boat river, meandering nearly twice the distance roads and railways need to reach its source on the lower slopes of the Cotswolds near Cirencester. Here, in a meadow beside the Tetbury road, a bearded, recumbent figure of Father Thames, sculptured in stone, marks the official beginning of the river's 210-mile (334 km.) journey to the sea. On its way it passes some of England's most visitable towns and villages and some of its most civilized scenery.

At Cricklade, a handsome, stone-built town on the Roman road to Cirencester, the adolescent Thames can support only canoes and shallow-draught dinghies but at Lechlade, ten miles (16 km.) below, sizeable launches can come up to the bridge. When St. Paul's Cathedral was being built in London, stone was loaded into barges here for the journey down the Thames.

The river from here to Dorchester is ambiguously known as 'Thames or Isis': the result of an age-old misunderstanding about the Roman name for the river, Thamesis, thought to be a combination of Thame and Isis. As a tributary, the Thame, joins the Thames at Dorchester, it was widely assumed that the river above Dorchester must be the Isis. The confusion need not worry anyone: the Thames by any other name flows just as sweet.

Threading its way through placid meadows, past Bablock Hythe, where the ferry claims to have been carrying men and their goods across the Thames for a thousand years, the river goes up to Oxford and finds a rival: the upstart Cherwell flowing in from Northamptonshire. Most of the University buildings lie between the two rivers but one of Oxford's most famous landmarks – Magdalen tower – is reflected in the waters of the Cherwell, not the Thames. The two join forces only south of the city, below Folly Bridge on the way to Abingdon, where the now dominant Thames glides through the town's triple bridge and past its magnificent Wren-style colonnaded Town Hall. At Dorchester the town's bridge crosses the Thame while the main river skirts the town, makes towards the Sinodun Hills, thinks better of it and turns sharply left to Wallingford, a town whose charter was granted by Henry II in 1155. Beyond the twin riverside towns of Streatley and Goring, the Thames is squeezed between the Chilterns and the Berkshire Downs – the Goring Gap – before coming to Pangbourne (of Nautical College fame) and Mapledurham (where 'Forsyte Saga' enthusiasts will probably remember the incident where

Soames was fatally injured by the falling picture).

Reading industrializes the scene for a brief stretch, quickly to return to the leisurely riverside life of Sonning (with its dazzling lockside flowers and water's-edge pubs), elegant Henley (home of the world-famous regatta), and Marlow (where the riverside hotel perpetuates Izaak Walton's classic book on the delights of fishing, 'The Compleat Angler'). Beyond Bourne End, Buckinghamshire's beechwoods cling to the steep eastern bank, camouflaging Cliveden, once the hill-top home of Lord Astor and now in the care of the National Trust. And then, through Maidenhead, to the goal of every Thames Valley visitor: Windsor Castle on its hill, dominating the skyline and keeping a parental eye on Eton College on the Buckinghamshire bank.

The charms of the Thames are so many and so evident that there is a danger of overlooking the more reticent attractions of the rest of the region. The Cotswold towns and villages with their honey-coloured stone houses and magnificent churches have a unique beauty, as has the Vale of White Horse, named after the prehistoric animal carved out of the chalk downs above Uffington. Off the beaten track, at Fair-

ford in Gloucestershire, the fifteenth century church has the most perfect and complete set of contemporary stained glass windows outside Westminster Abbey and King's College Chapel.

The Chilterns, beside glorious windswept views, harbour delectable villages like Fingest in its deep green valley and slightly self-conscious Long Crendon, one of England's many 'picture

postcard' villages. Whipsnade Zoo clings to the green hillsides of Dunstable Downs and in the air above them gliders soar on the strong thermal currents. Essex, to the east, often dismissed as 'flat' has new towns to show at Harlow and Basildon as well as a hundred villages unchanged for centuries with names that one feels should be set to music.

Opposite, above: Windsor, as a site for a royal castle, was chosen by William the Conqueror not, as you might think, for the beauty of its setting but for the security it provided. It was on a chalk hill to give all-round visibility; the Thames formed a natural moat; the Tower of London was only a day's march away; it was adjacent to the royal hunting grounds of Windsor Forest. As a result of these largely defensive considerations the castle has only twice been besieged in close on 1000 years: once when Prince John rebelled against Richard I and occupied it; and again by the Barons when John had become king. During the Civil War it was in the hands of the Parliamentary troops; the Lady-chapel was used as a powder magazine and the castle as a prison. The Round Tower dates from the twelfth century but most of the outer parts of the castle were built in the time of George IV.

Opposite below: The sixteenth century gatehouse and quadrangle of Corpus Christi College, Oxford, are shown here. The college was founded in 1516 by Bishop Richard Fox, a close friend of Bishop Oldham, the founder of Manchester Grammar School. The unusual obelisk in the middle of the quadrangle is a sundial given to the college in 1581 by Charles Turnbull. The actual dial, which is near

the top of the pillar, is surmounted by a pelican (the badge of Corpus Christi) and below there is a perpetual calendar.

Above: Through the early morning mist Blenheim Palace looms up – 'the most splendid relic of the age of Anne', as the ninth Duke of Marlborough called it. And splendid it is in spite of all the ill-feeling that arose over its building. After the Duke of Marlborough's famous victory at the Battle of Blenheim, Queen Anne, on behalf of a grateful nation, presented him with the Royal Manor of Woodstock and the promise of a grant of £240,000 towards building Blenheim Palace. Endless feuds broke out principally between Sarah, the first Duchess, and Sir John Vanbrugh, the architect, and funds began to prove inadequate. The Duke finally had to contribute some £60,000 out of his own pocket. Ironically he died before its completion. Ten years after his death an elaborate memorial to the Duke, carried out by Rysbrack at a cost of £2200, was unveiled. The small photograph (left) shows a detail from only a portion of the base. Sir Robert Walpole, on being taken to a service in the chapel and seeing the memorial, is said to have enquired innocently whether they had come to worship God or the Duke of Marlborough.

Left : Crossing Icknield Way, the pre-historic track
that runs from Dorchester to Thetford in Norfolk,
Britwell Hill climbs past a field of mustard up to
the sun-flecked beech woods of the Chilterns. This
is perfect walking and riding country, cross-stitched
with footpaths and bridleways and opening up wide-
eyed views across the Vale of Aylesbury to Oxford.
Several hundred acres (about 100 hectares) of
Chiltern beech woods, given mainly by Viscount
Esher's family since the last war, are now in the care
of the National Trust.

Above : The Fourth of June at Eton College is an annual holiday instituted by George III to celebrate his birthday. The procession of boats on the Thames is a traditional feature of the day and the 'wet-bobs', as the oarsmen at Eton are known, dress as sailors of George III's time and wear flowers round their hats. During the procession, stroke and bow remain seated and row while the rest of the eight stand with their oars raised. Cox's job – he is in full naval officer's uniform with sword – must indeed be quite a tricky one.

Left : Cricket began on the village greens of England and it is on the village greens that the game still enjoys its most popular support. Here, at Hill Green near the beautiful Essex town of Saffron Walden, the village team enjoys the luxury of a modern, thatched pavilion. An added refinement, not enjoyed by many village clubs, is the pavilion clock to remind the players that time is not always on their side.

Above : The Thames locks are convivial meeting places as well as a means of getting up and down the river without 'shooting' the weirs. Most of them are immaculately kept with brightly painted lock-keeper's houses and gardens full of summer flowers. The lock at Goring is on a particularly busy stretch of the river with Goring on the Oxfordshire bank and the popular Swan Inn at Streatley on the Berkshire side and connecting them the Goring bridge.

THE SOUTH-EASTERN
❧ COUNTIES ❧

THE SOUTH-EAST has always been England's front door, nowadays open and welcoming but, in the past, often slammed shut in the face of enemies. Through it came the Celts bringing the Iron Age with them. Uninvited came the Romans imposing their materialistic civilization on the country and pushing the Celts out into its western fringes. The Anglo-Saxons followed leaving their churches and literature to mark their passage. When the Normans invaded in 1066 they, too, came through England's front door, landing at Pevensey Bay, winning a decisive battle behind Hastings, and then marching around Kent to London where William built the Tower and tamed the country with sword and fire. Spain's Armada never reached the front door, had barely got to the front gate before being decimated by British sea power and gales. Napoleon and Hitler both looked enviously across the Channel at 'the white cliffs of Dover' and quailed at the prospect of landing on so unfriendly a shore.

These same white cliffs, which are many people's first sight of England – at Dover or Newhaven – are the sliced-off ends of two ranges of chalk hills that delimit the region: the North and South Downs. Between them lies so much beautiful country and so many interesting places

that visitors to Britain often travel no further.

At either end of this region stand the two great cathedrals of Canterbury and Winchester – Canterbury where Thomas à Becket was murdered and Winchester where King Alfred was buried. Between the two and running along the ridge of the North Downs are the remains of a Bronze Age track which was almost certainly the main east-west trade route in ancient times. But after the murder of Becket in 1170 and his subsequent canonization, so many pilgrims going to Canterbury used the route that parts of it have become traditionally known as the Pilgrim's Way. One of the best places to locate it is just south-east of Guildford where St. Martha's church stands independent of any village on a spur of the Downs. The old track runs past the church which is thought to have been the site of a chantry chapel and from it there is a view that epitomizes southern England: tree upon tree, field after field, hill and hollow for 25 miles (40 km.) to the south where, on a clear day, the mushroom shape of Chanctonbury Ring may be seen. This grove of trees planted in the eighteenth century on the site of an Iron Age earthwork is as much a landmark on the South Downs as St. Martha's is on the North. To match the

Left: Canterbury is the heart of Christian England. Where the cathedral stands a church was consecrated five years after St. Augustine arrived from Rome to re-Christianize England in 597 A.D. Nothing of this Saxon church survives and only the foundations of the Norman cathedral begun in 1070 are to be seen. After a disastrous fire in 1174 the cathedral was virtually rebuilt and extended to include a shrine for St. Thomas à Becket, murdered on the steps of the north transept in 1170. This shrine became England's most important place of pilgrimage. The 'Bell Harry' tower, which dominates Canterbury's skyline today is relatively modern – a mere 500 years old.

Right: Rye's cobbled Mermaid Street is typical of this little town which clings to a lump of red sandstone protruding from the flat of Romney Marsh. Now nearly two miles (3 km.) from the sea, it was one of the two 'Ancient Towns' associated with the Cinque Ports and an important naval base during the Hundred Years War. Though its hill may have saved Rye from inundation from the sea, it did not save it from a ferocious attack by the French in

1377 when the town was left 'a smouldering ruin'.
Henry James, the celebrated American novelist,
came to live in Rye in 1897, occupying Lamb House
until his death in 1916. Part of the house is open to
visitors.

Above: There is nothing in England quite like the
Sussex Downs, a long range of chalk hills, almost
devoid of features but full of charm and personality.
Every crest presents a view of the sea or the Weald,
every valley shelters some delightful village. Along
their length the South Downs Way runs for some
80 miles (130 km.), providing a traffic-free bridle-
way for walkers, riders and cyclists. The photograph shows the Downs near Berwick, between
Eastbourne and Lewes.

Left: The Seven Sisters are a series of seven peaks in the chalk cliff between Birling Gap and Cuckmere Haven on the Sussex coast – a precipitous ending to the South Downs. Each Sister has a name, though they are far from feminine. From the right they are: Went Hill Brow, Baily's Hill, Flagstaff Point, Bran Point, Rough Brow, Short Brow and Haven Brow. For many visitors crossing the Channel they are the first sight of England.

Below: Bosham is an attractive waterside village with a spired church that is 'the oldest site of Christianity in Sussex'. The waterfront road is regularly flooded at high tide – a fact which supports the belief that it was at Bosham that King Canute proved that the waves were no respecter of royal authority.

Pilgrim's Way along the North Downs, a South Downs Way has now been designated and mapped. It can be followed (on foot only) from Beachy Head for 80 miles (130 km.) almost to Petersfield.

The south-east has the most popular and populous sea coast in the whole of Britain. Londoners flock to the north Kent resorts such as Herne Bay, Margate and Broadstairs where sand, sea and sunshine still form the firm basis for a day at the seaside. The other south-coast resorts, stretching from Ramsgate to Bournemouth offer every variation between the slightly formal elegance of Eastbourne and the occasional stretch of coast almost unmarked by civilization.

If it is sunshine that you are wanting, the Isle of Wight claims the most.

One notable exception to the chain of seaside resorts is that stretch of the coast between Winchelsea and Hythe known as Romney Marsh, its inland boundary marked by the line of the Royal Military Canal – a leftover from the Napoleonic wars as are the Martello towers that dot this coast. Sheep graze purposefully where the sea once gave access to the Cinque Ports of Romney, Hythe, Winchelsea and Rye. Today they are charming little towns some distance from the sea and with a character quite different from that of the rest of the coast.

Surprisingly there is a coal-mining area

between Canterbury and Deal but apart from this and the industrial sprawl that spreads out from Southampton and Portsmouth the region retains an astonishingly rural profile. For instance, Tunbridge Wells – now a town of some 50,000 people – retains its rocky, wooded centre in which Queen Henrietta Maria camped for six weeks in 1630 while taking the waters discovered a few years earlier by Lord North. In Guildford too – an even larger town – the green meadows of the Wey valley still reach right into its heart. The length and breadth of the region there are enchanting small towns such as Tenterden, Goudhurst, Arundel and Lewes where the architectural styles of several centuries co-exist with

Left: Chartwell, Sir Winston Churchill's former home, two miles south of Westerham on the Kentish Weald, is only of minor architectural interest (it was virtually rebuilt when he bought it in 1923) but no house in the world manages to convey so much of the essence of its former owner. Particularly is this true of his study, shown here as it is today – almost exactly as he left it for the last time in October 1964. From the rafters hangs a replica of his banner as a knight of the Order of the Garter. The British flag over the fireplace was flown above the first European city to be liberated in the Second World War. The large picture is of Blenheim Palace where he was born in 1874. The photographs on the wall include Queen Elizabeth II, a favourite portrait of his father Lord Randolph Churchill, and Franklin Roosevelt. In addition to the many family portraits on his desk, there are busts of Nelson and Napoleon and a polished marble eagle. On the small round table by his armchair is the ever-present

modern developments in reasonable harmony.

The villages of the south-east too are quite outstanding: Fordwich, east of Canterbury, where the stones for the cathedral, brought across the Channel from Caen, were unloaded; Shere, astride the Tillingbourne in Surrey; East Meon at the head of the Meon valley in Hampshire; and the unspoilt village of Cuckfield in Sussex. Going back further in time there are important Roman remains at Dover and at Fishbourne just west of Chichester, where a third century palace is gradually being revealed as the excavations continue. And, jumping forward in time, who, while in the region, would willingly miss a visit to Chartwell, the highly individual and powerfully evocative home of the man who did more than most to slam the south-east's door in Hitler's face: Sir Winston Churchill.

Right: In 1785, at the time of his morganatic marriage to Mrs. Fitzherbert, and when he was deeply in debt, the Prince of Wales, later George IV, decided to economize by closing his London home and living the frugal life in Brighton. At first he leased a modest house which he later bought but he liked Brighton so much that he had the house pulled down and got Henry Holland to build him a much more elaborate establishment: the Marine Pavilion. This was enlarged as his circle of friends expanded, but the Prince had grander ideas and, in 1811, when he became Prince Regent, he embarked on the Royal Pavilion much as it is today. With its Indian exterior and Chinese interior it is without doubt one of the world's most elaborate fantasies – and it was designed by John Nash, the architect of many of the most elegant parts of Regency London.

box of cigars (he is said to have smoked 3,000 a year). The working desk on the right (he often wrote standing) was a gift from his children. The carpet was a sixty-ninth birthday present from the Shah of Persia.

The house is in a lovely position on a hillside and his studio, still full of his vigorous paintings, is in the garden. The National Trust now looks after Chartwell and it is open to the public.

Right: Sir Richard Baker built Sissinghurst Castle in Kent, an Elizabethan courtyard house and entertained the Queen there in 1573. A tall brick tower is all that is now left of the original building. It is now one of the National Trust's many properties but, until a few years ago, it was the home of Sir Harold Nicolson and his wife, the writer and poet Victoria (Vita) Sackville-West. When they first bought the property in 1930 it was a wilderness. Together they planned and planted a series of small gardens each one devoted to an individual theme.

They turned Sissinghurst into one of the show-gardens of England. One feature is the informal planting of roses, mainly the old-fashioned shrub varieties. The gardens and the tower are open to the public.

❧ THE WEST COUNTRY ❧

WRITING IN BRIEF about the West Country is like writing a precis of the 'Encyclopaedia Britannica' or summarizing the contents of the British Museum. Something has to give: the problem is not what to put in but what to leave out. Cathedrals for instance; Salisbury, Exeter and Wells cannot be ignored and even Truro, the nineteenth century creation of J. Loughborough Pearson, deserves more than the dismissive tag of 'a piece of Early English revival'. And if cathedrals cannot be left out, what about all those wonderful churches, from the early Anglo-Saxon church of St. Lawrence, Bradford-on-Avon to the neo-Byzantine splendour of St. Osmund's, Parkstone. Houses, too, must be included. Penfound Manor, one of the oldest inhabited manor houses in Britain, was mentioned in the Domesday Book; Cotehele, an early sixteenth century Cornish manor house, almost unchanged since it was built; Saltram House, near Plymouth, with its superb Robert Adam interiors; and Wiltshire's Lacock Abbey dating from the fourteenth century with the adjoining Lacock village totally preserved by the National Trust. Castles range from the purely defensive like Portland, Dartmouth or Pendennis to the more domestic, lived-in castles like Compton Castle, occupied by the descendants of Sir Humphrey Gilbert since the sixteenth century, or Castle Drogo, probably the last building of its kind ever to be built in Britain, designed by Sir Edwin Lutyens and standing over 900 feet (274 m.) up overlooking a gorge of the river Teign.

At least the West Country is readily definable: a slightly devious line joining Gloucester and Southampton satisfies most people as to its eastern border; the sea ordains the boundaries north and south; and Land's End places its final full-stop to the west. It is the characterization of this west-pointing peninsula that poses the next problem. Scenically the chalk uplands of Salisbury Plain have little in common with the granite crags of Cornwall's Penwith Peninsula, yet both share man's pre-historic puzzles. While Stonehenge is probably the most celebrated stone circle in Europe, few will be familiar with a similar circle though on a very different scale: the 'Merry Maidens' of St. Buryan. Equally they stand silent and mysterious, challenging us to unravel their meaning.

Above: Where the red cliffs of Devon advancing eastwards change dramatically to chalk-white, the village of Beer nestles in its east-facing corner of Seaton Bay. Here the sea is deep, clear and inviting but an eight-knot current round Beer Head makes swimming from the pebbly beach something to be undertaken with proper care. When westerly gales are pounding south-facing beaches, Beer fishermen can launch their boats in comparative safety. Lace-making is the village's traditional craft, though smuggling was once its more profitable occupation.

Right: Polperro has become such a tourist magnet that it is difficult to realize that it was once a quiet, self-sufficient fishing harbour with no sounds but the mew of gulls and no smell but that of freshly landed fish and salt sea air. Though it now leads something of a transitory life of car parks, popcorn and pin-tables, it is still a beautiful little place. Its slate-roofed houses are steeply stacked above the double harbour where persistent wavelets slap against the sides of the vermilion, violet and turquoise boats that nod at anchor. Visit Polperro, if possible, at any time but high summer.

If the West Country is rich in pre-historic relics it is richer still in the myths and legends that surround them. Tintagel thrives on the quite insupportable claim that King Arthur was born there in the sixth century; the ruins on the cliff edge date from at least six centuries later. There are more genuine grounds for believing that Cadbury Castle in Somerset might have been the site of Arthur's Camelot. Glastonbury, also in Somerset, is the legendary burial place of King Arthur and the spot where Joseph of Arimathea, having transported the Holy Grail from Jerusalem, struck his staff into the ground where it took root and grew into the Holy Thorn bush which flowers each Christmas Day.

While the legends of the West Country are fascinating the landscapes are superb and very real. Each of the five counties, Cornwall, Devon, Somerset, Dorset and Wiltshire, has its wilderness though some are wilder than others. Wildest of all is Devon's Dartmoor, officially designated one of Britain's national parks and covering over 350 square miles (900 sq. km.). Its granite uplands were extensively inhabited in the Bronze and Iron Ages as the remains of the many stone hut circles prove, but today, apart from a few villages close to the crossing roads, and Her Majesty's Prison at Princetown, it is deserted except for wild deer and ponies. Walkers, other than experienced cross-country navigators, are wise to keep to the roads or well-trodden tracks.

The two highest points in Cornwall, Brown Willy (1375 feet/417 m.) and Rough Tor (1311 feet/400 m.) are found close to each other on Bodmin Moor, a high granite-strewn area lying between the upper reaches of the rivers Inny and Camel. There is only one road across the moor and it was the appalling state of this road in the seventeenth century that prevented Bodmin from then becoming the county town of Cornwall: the assize judges could not be persuaded to venture further west than Launceston. If they had they would have discovered, as millions of holidaymakers have, that the true glory of the West Country is the long and magnificent sea coast that borders this pointing finger of land. From Weston-super-Mare and the Severn Estuary right round to Hengistbury Head and the Needles (now in the safe custody of the National Trust) there are cliff walks and beaches, sheltered bays and quiet coves, headlands, harbours,

Above: Less than half of the New Forest is trees. For the rest this former royal hunting ground is a delightful mixture of open heathland, pasture, farms and villages. Only 'commoners' – people who live within the forest boundaries – are allowed to graze their animals in the forest and the New Forest ponies, though they may appear to be wild, are all privately owned. Each year a number are rounded up and sold at pony fairs. One such fair is held at Swan Green, the village shown in this picture.

Below: Below Bonehill Down on the eastern side of Dartmoor, Widecombe crouches in the broad valley through which the East Webburn river flows on its way to join the Dart. Beyond, to the west, is the wild expanse of the Dartmoor of heather-covered moorland and rocky outcrops where inexperienced walkers can easily lose their way. But here, around Widecombe, the land is more fertile, as the cultivated field pattern shows. The 'Widdicombe' Fair, per-petuated in the song, to which Uncle Tom Cobbleigh and his friends wanted to ride on Tom Pearse's grey mare, is held on the second Tuesday in Sep-tember. Widecombe's beautiful fourteenth century granite church with its tall pinnacled tower is known as 'the cathedral of the moor'.

Right: South of the Bath road between Froxfield and Marlborough, Savernake Forest's 16-mile (26-km.) circumference encircles some 2,000 acres (800 hectares) of stately forest trees – mainly huge oaks and beeches. The forest has been Crown property ever since the Norman Conquest and is managed by the Forestry Commission but the public can freely wander along its magnificent avenues and rides and it is a splendid place in which to picnic. It is also a good place to see rare birds and wildflowers.

Following pages: There is a finality about the very words 'Land's End' that is not shared by Spain's 'Finisterre' or the legendary 'Ultima Thule'. Here England really does end, where the tip of the West Country's finger is savagely manicured by the endless impact of the Atlantic. Nothing but 3000 miles (5000 km.) of ocean, as the Pilgrim Fathers knew only too well, lies between Land's End and the North American continent. Even the plethora of 'last pubs', 'last shops', 'last filling stations' and 'last post boxes' cannot seriously detract from the grandeur of the westward scene, especially early in the morning or when the sun is bouncing on the far horizon.

creeks, estuaries, seaside towns and villages that make this whole region Britain's unique holiday haven. Its climate, too, is softer, warmer and more equable than the rest of Britain and along the south coast 'Riviera', from Falmouth to Dawlish, palm trees flourish and sub-tropical plants grow freely.

For lovers of marine drama the many headlands on the north Cornish coast provide grandstand views when Atlantic gales bring thousands of tons of boiling seas crashing down on to the unyielding rocks and, when the storm has abated, the same Atlantic rollers carry surfers far up the wide sandy beaches of Newquay, Bude, Westward Ho! and Saunton Sands. For yachtsmen the more sheltered south coasts with their wide bays and deep estuaries offer not only safe sailing but also friendly harbours and magnificent coastal scenery.

Above: Bath's Pulteney Bridge, built in 1771 to the design of Robert Adam, serves the dual purpose of a covered arcade of shops and a bridge across the river Avon. Bath's mineral springs were first recognized by the Romans who established their settlement of Aquae Sulis here in A.D. 44, but the city's greatest period of growth, both physically and socially, was in Georgian times under the influence of Beau Nash. He was a penniless Welsh lad who

became Bath's Master of Ceremonies, cleaned the place up, installed street lighting, had the Pump Room and Assembly Rooms built, drew up rules of social behaviour and generally transformed a small country town into an elegant and influential city.

Right: Lacock Abbey, three miles (5 km.) south of Chippenham in Wiltshire, was founded in 1229 as a house of Augustinian canonesses. It was one of the last to be dissolved because there was 'no fault to be found with these ladies'. However, Henry VIII had his way and the place was bought in 1540 for £763 by Sir William Sharington and converted into a Tudor mansion, many of the features of which are still preserved. In the early eighteenth century the abbey came into the possession of the Talbot family whose descendants lived there until 1958 when it passed to the National Trust. It was here in 1839 that William Fox Talbot perfected the negative-positive system which has made modern photography possible. This leaded-light window was the subject of his first – and world-famous – photographic print.

Far right: Wells Cathedral is the cathedral of the diocese of Bath and Wells. The unique feature of the cathedral's interior is the crossing arch, in the form of a truncated figure-of-eight, placed beneath the central tower in 1338 to prevent its threatened collapse. Another architectural feature of Wells is the delicately beautiful octagonal chapter house.

The cathedral's greatest glory is the west front, a stone screen containing some 400 separate statues and flanked by two sturdy towers, all added by Bishop Jocelyn early in the thirteenth century. The cathedral clock, at least 600 years old, is a masterpiece of mechanical ingenuity – and ingenious, too, are the swans on the Bishop's moat who have for years rung a bell for their dinner.

❧ NORTH WALES ❧

To an englishman the attraction of a visit to Wales is the attraction of going to a 'foreign' country without crossing water or changing money or needing a passport, for the Welsh are a separate people with their own language, customs and characteristics, and with deep national aspirations to run their own affairs in their own way in their own country. No one could feel more 'abroad' than when standing in the parlour of an inn at, say, Beaumaris in Anglesey, surrounded by a throng of Welshmen chatting together. Unless he happens to know some Gaelic or Celtic words, not one syllable

Chepstow and long stretches of it are visible today. It was built not so much as a defence as a boundary – a boundary to separate the Celts of Wales from the Anglo-Saxons of England. But it was such a formidable boundary that not only did it keep the Celts out of England but it also kept the English out of Wales. Gradually these strangers in the other world beyond Offa's Dyke became known as the Welsh, a word derived from the Anglo-Saxon for 'foreigners' and, to the English at any rate, 'foreigners' they have remained with their different looks, different temperaments, different and unpronounceable

will sound familiar to his ears (as it might in France or Italy) and the manner of speaking will have an excitement and emphasis which most Englishmen deliberately avoid.

This separateness began in the eighth century A.D. when King Offa of Mercia built the dyke that bears his name. It ran from Prestatyn on the Dee in the north to the Severn estuary near

language and ability to sing not only in tune but in perfect, natural harmony.

What the Welsh have always preserved – perhaps because of their isolation – is the innate Celtic hospitality. Nowhere in the world, once a man has established his own authenticity, will he be made more genuinely welcome. And to a stranger in a strange land little is more important.

Anticipating the Welshness of Wales, the visitor entering the country on the northern coast road from Chester may be disappointed to note how 'English' Colwyn Bay, Rhyl and Prestatyn have become under the influence of holiday-makers from the north of England. The mood changes noticeably at Llandudno, a rather elegant resort nestling between the two Ormes Heads – Great and Little. 'Llan' is the commonest prefix in Welsh place names and is the Welsh word for 'church', so it was appropriate that it should have been at Llandudno – 'the church of Tudno' – that the Rev. Charles Dodgson, better known as Lewis Carroll, first met Alice Liddell whom he immortalized in Alice in Wonderland.

From Great Ormes Head, whose 679-foot (207 m.) summit may be reached by railway or cable-car, there is a spectacular panoramic view which takes in Snowdonia, Anglesey, the Isle of Man and the Lakeland peaks. From Bangor the main road crosses Thomas Telford's 1000-foot (304-m.) long suspension bridge built in 1826 and arrives in Anglesey close to a village that is famous only for the 58 letters of its name: Llanfairpwllgwyngyllgogerychwyrndrobwll-llantysiliogogogoch. It is spelt out in full on the

Left: The massive and wonderfully preserved bulk of Conway Castle makes the modern road bridge over the Conway estuary an insignificant feat of engineering in comparison. The castle was built by Edward I 700 years ago as a means of maintaining English dominance over Llywelyn, the last – and most independent – of the independent Welsh princes. The handsome road bridge, which fits in so well with the medieval scene, was built in 1958 to relieve the growing weight of traffic using Thomas Telford's famous 1826 suspension bridge which was designed on the same lines as his suspension bridge over the Menai Strait and opened in the same year. The third bridge over the Conway – Robert Stephenson's tubular rail bridge of 1848 – tried hard to harmonize with its spectacular surroundings by introducing 'Gothic' towers. The town walls, of which the castle forms the most easterly point, are remarkably complete with 21 semi-circular defensive towers and a total length of half a mile (805 m.).
Far left: Lake Bala is the largest natural lake in Wales (some of the man-made reservoir lakes are larger). It is four miles (6.4 km.) long, up to three-quarters of a mile (1.2 km.) wide, 150 feet (46 m.) deep at its deepest point, a busy sailing and fishing centre and the scene of British Long Distance Swimming Championships. At the north end of the lake is the little town of Bala, an excellent tourist centre. with a treelined main street and some good hotels. The valley of the river Dee, which flows into lake Bala, is surrounded by three mountain groups which provide spectacular scenery. From the lakeside in Bala, the peaks of Aran Benllyn and Cader Idris, both nudging 3000 feet (900 m.), can be seen. Tradition says that the waters of the river Dee never mingle with those of the lake. Like most Welsh lakes, Bala has its legend and there is a drowned palace beneath this one.

Right: At the meeting point of two rivers and three valleys, in the heart of Snowdonia and in the shadow of Moel Hebog (Hawk Hill, 2566 feet/780 m.) is Beddgelert, a compact and delightful centre for touring in this spectacular region. The name Beddgelert means grave of Gelert, and there is some confusion about who Gelert, or Celert, was. He was probably Celert, a British saint of the sixth century, but an enterprising landlord of the Royal Goat Inn in the early nineteenth century had a much better idea. There is a story that Gelert was the favourite and trusted hound of Prince Llywelyn. One day he left the dog to guard his infant son and returned to be greeted by the animal covered in blood. In a moment of fury he slew the dog only to discover that Gelert had killed a wolf that was trying to attack the child, and that his son was unharmed. There the legend would have ended until the enterprising landlord erected a primitive cairn in the meadow below Cerrig Llan and commissioned a ballad-monger to write a song and spread the tale that it was the grave of Gelert. As time passed, the cairn became a popular place of pilgrimage – and Beddgelert benefited.

Left : Wales is rich in railways – particularly the narrow-gauge steam trains mostly run by devoted bands of railway enthusiasts. There are eight such lines in north- and mid-Wales. The exception to this amateur status is the highly professional Snowdon Mountain Railway, the only rack railway in the British Isles.

From its terminus at Llanberis in Caernarvonshire the single coach trains climb 4½ miles (7.44 kms) up the 2 ft 7½ ins (80 cms) gauge track to a point just below the 3560 foot (1085 m) summit of Snowdon – an average gradient of 1 in 6.86. For safety's sake a maximum speed of 5 m.p.h. (8.5 km.p.h.) is observed which means that the round journey takes almost two hours but provides magnificent views across North Wales to Anglesey, the Isle of Man and even to Ireland on a clear day.

The four engines which operate the service were built in Switzerland over eighty years ago but are as sprightly as ever.

Below : This picture shows a hillside scene near Bala. One of the best books on Wales – perhaps one of the best travel books ever written – was George Borrow's 'Wild Wales' first published in 1862.

His description of his approach to Bala makes a fitting caption to this picture. 'Shortly after leaving the village of the tollgate I came to a beautiful valley. On my right hand was a river, the farther bank of which was fringed with trees; on my left was a gentle ascent, the lower part of which was covered with yellow luxuriant corn; a little farther on was a green grove, behind which rose up a moel [bare, rounded hill]. A more bewitching scene I have never beheld. Ceres and Pan seemed in this place to have met to hold their bridal. The sun now descending shone nobly on the whole.'

railway station, a garage and a newsagent's but generally it is abbreviated to Llanfair PG. Anglesey lacks only mountains. It is a beautiful, rugged and productive island with numberless sandy beaches and bays. The island must have been a popular place in pre-historic times judging by the wealth of archaeological remains.

On the mainland across the Menai Strait, Snowdon is the great natural feature. For those who do not wish to climb it (it is little more than a challenging walk) or go up to its 3,560-foot (1085-m.) peak on the mountain railway from Llanberis, the classic road tour is from Caernarvon to Llanberis, over the Llanberis Pass, turn right to Beddgelert and right again to Caernarvon – a trip of about 30 miles (48 km.). Snowdon is the centre of the Snowdonia National Park – 845 square miles (2,200 sq. km.) of countryside preserved against unsuitable development and stretching from Llanberis in the north to the Dovey estuary on Cardigan Bay to the south. To the west, the Lleyn peninsula, the picturesque upper arm of Cardigan Bay, pushes out into the Irish Sea, protecting a chain of characterful seaside towns and villages that ring the bay: Abersoch, Llanbedrog, Pwllheli,

Criccieth, Portmadoc, Portmeirion, Harlech, Barmouth, Tywyn, Aberdovey and Aberystwyth. There is a panoramic walk from Barmouth up the Mawddach river to Dolgellau. From it there are grand mountain views of Cader Idris and Craig Lwyd, its summit. Further south, beyond Machynlleth, the Plynlimon range marks the source of the Severn and the Wye.

The countryside between Machynlleth and Welshpool, near the English border is high moorland, little visited and only thinly inhabited but beautiful in a wild way; further north, however, the Vale of Llangollen is green and tree-filled. Llangollen itself is famous for its annual Eisteddfod which attracts competitors from 30 countries throughout the world. Famous too, is Plas Newydd, the mansion home for 50 years of the 'Ladies of Llangollen', two eccentric spinsters, Lady Eleanor Butler and Miss Sarah Ponsonby, whose graves can be seen in the churchyard of St. Collen's. Llangollen quite recently achieved a new distinction when the Prince of Wales presented the British Tourist Authority's 'Come to Britain' Trophy to the proprietors of Llangollen's Canal Exhibition Centre.

Right : Caernarvon is another of Edward I's castles built to dominate the newly-subdued Welsh, though it was not begun until after Prince Llywelyn's death. It is even larger and more imposing than Conway and is generally said to be the most magnificent in Britain except perhaps Alnwick in Northumberland. The castle walls are between seven and nine feet (2.1 and 2.7 m.) thick and they enclose some three acres (or 1 hectare). There are stirring views across the Menai Straits to Anglesey and inland to Snowdonia. Snowdon itself is only eight miles (13 km.) away. Within the castle is the fascinating regimental museum of the Royal Welsh Fusiliers and, in the Castle Square, a statue of David Lloyd George, the most prominent Welshman of this century. Prince Charles' investiture in Caernarvon Castle in 1969 was a re-enactment of a ceremony which first took place almost 700 years ago when the future Edward II was presented to the Welsh people as the first Prince of Wales. Rather wittily Edward I announced that he was, as promised, presenting them with a prince 'unable to speak English'. The prince was only a few months old at the time.

Right: The transference of an architectural idiom from one country to another is rarely successful, and to do so from the drenching sunlight of Italy to the greyer skies of Wales would seem to be courting disaster. Yet Portmeirion, on a wooded peninsula between Harlech and Portmadog, has obstinately succeeded. It began in 1926 when the Welsh architect Clough Williams-Ellis set out to prove that 'development' need not result in spoliation. His inspiration was Portofino in Italy and he visualized Portmeirion as a living exhibition of the varied architecture and landscaping of the Italian village. It may have become something of a museum but it is a very interesting and splendid one. Visitors are charged a small entrance fee in order to keep it that way.

Left: Abersoch is a most attractive village at the mouth of the river Soch within the sheltering arm of Cardigan Bay. Sailing is the great attraction here and, in the summer months, the estuary and the waters of the bay are alive with coloured sails. The two off-shore islands of St. Trudwal are the home of guillemots and puffins, and a favourite haunt of bird-watchers. The islands were bought in 1934 by Clough Williams-Ellis, the architect, to save them from development.

❧ SOUTH WALES ❧

ANY VISITING SPECTATOR at a Llanelli v. Swansea rugby match would find it hard to believe that he was in what was once the most 'English' part of Wales. Yet many of the southern towns – Chepstow, Cardiff, Caerphilly, Swansea, Newport, Llanelli, Carmarthen, Pembroke and Haverfordwest – grew out of mainly English settlements around the castles built by the marauding Norman barons. The indigenous Welsh retreated into the hills and valleys, rebelling from time to time but not returning to claim their own until the Industrial Revolution and its demand for labour in the coal mines and ironworks attracted them back to a new form of serfdom.

Today the Welshmen of South Wales may not be quite as vociferously Welsh-speaking as their brothers and sisters in the north, but they share all the other good qualities of Welshmen everywhere including their aptitude for singing and their ready hospitality. In one thing they excel: their devotion to rugby football.

The southern half of Wales is a very beautiful land of mountains (though not as high as those in the north) lakes, waterfalls and rivers; of superb coastal scenery, especially on the Pembroke coast; with two National Parks covering hundreds of unspoilt square miles; with some fine Roman remains at Caerleon and Caerwent; with castles and monasteries both ruined and working; and the valleys, many sadly scarred

Left: Where the river Wye marks the boundary between Wales and England at Monmouth, it is joined by a tributary, the Monow. And on the Monow bridge is this fortified gateway added to the Norman bridge in 1260 to form one of the four medieval gateways into the town. Ever since the union of Wales and England there has been some ambiguity about the position of Monmouthshire. Official documents avoided decisiveness by referring to 'Wales and Monmouthshire'. Ordnance survey maps designated it part of England. Now that the administrative counties have been reorganized, Monmouthshire's position has been made clear: it is no longer Monmouthshire – it has had bits chopped off and added on and been renamed Gwent, and there is no doubt about that being Welsh.

Right: Llangorse lake lies seven miles (11 km.) north-east of the Brecon Beacons on the northern boundary of the Brecon Beacons National Park. It is the largest natural lake in South Wales and, like Bala its counterpart in the north, legends insist that its waters cover a buried community, in this case the town of Mara. The name Llangorse means 'church in a fen' and although the lake is set among reed beds, it is hardly a fen. It is a regular nesting place for great crested grebes, little grebes, coots, goosanders and red-breasted mergansers. The lake is a popular recreational centre and attracts boating enthusiasts of all kinds as well as fishermen determined to hook its outsize eels, perch and pike.

because of the wealth of coal that lay beneath them, but now greening over again and still lovely on the upper slopes.

Wales, being a country of relatively high rainfall and finding itself with more water than it needs, has come to a more or less amicable arrangement to export its surplus to England. Birmingham, for instance, draws the bulk of its water supply from the lovely Elan Valley, west of Rhayader in what used to be Radnorshire (now part of Powys). The first dams were built at the end of the nineteenth century and the latest after the Second World War. The enormous artificial lakes that now occupy the valleys have become a major tourist attraction in an area that was once one of the remotest in Wales. The poet Shelley brought his 16-year-old wife, Harriet West-

brook, to live in the valley. Cwmlan, their home for a few unconventional months, lies at the bottom of one of the reservoirs. One farmhouse, typical of those in the valley which were about to be submerged, was dismantled and rebuilt in the National Folk Museum at St. Fagan's near Cardiff.

Further south, around the town of Brecon, the Brecon Beacons National Park spreads its largely unspoilt and well-cared-for countryside over 519 square miles (1300 sq. km.) of South Wales. Its scenery varies from the truly natural of the mountains – a landscape ladled out in generous, solidified helpings – to the carefully tailored fields of the farms in the green valleys below.

Many rivers rise in the National Park area,

some joining the Wye or the Usk while others, less well-known, make their way to the Bristol Channel through the industrial valleys and towns. Because of industrial pollution to the lower reaches of the rivers, most of the South Wales towns now draw their water from the 16 reservoirs high up on the southern edge of the Park. Cardiff, for example, is served by a reservoir in the Taf Fawr valley and Swansea water comes from Talybont. These reservoir-lakes, like those in the Elan valley, add greatly to the scenic pleasures of the park area.

The Brecon Beacons themselves swell out of the landscape like breakers arching from the sea. The highest crest, Pen y Fan (2906 feet/883 m.), drops a precipitous 600 feet (182 m.) on its northern face. To the south the Beacons slope

Opposite page: Caerphilly Castle is over 700 years old and, after Windsor, the largest in Europe. During its early years it was repeatedly destroyed and rebuilt and, in the seventeenth century, Cromwell's troops blasted its famous leaning tower nine feet out of the perpendicular. Though much restoration work has been done on the castle in recent years, this tower has been allowed to remain leaning.

Top: The outer, castellated buildings of Cardiff Castle, were created by William Burges in 1861 for the third Marquess of Bute; they include buildings in the Gothic, Arab and Classical Greek styles and follow the outline of the eight-acre walled enclosure of an earlier Roman fort. Within the grounds is a fine example of a Norman keep, built by Robert Fitz-Hamon, one of the noble marauders whom William the Conqueror sent into Wales. The original

motte is surmounted by the keep whose outer walls contain stone from the Roman fortification.

Left: Remove the bell-turret from this little church at Capel-y-ffin in Monmouthshire and there is one of the little white-washed cottages that dot the hillsides of this thinly inhabited area where Monmouthshire, Breconshire (now Gwent and Powys) and Herefordshire meet. The churchyard is full of ancient yews and solemn gravestones. A visiting clergyman in the 1870s described the church in his diary as 'short, stout and boxy'.

Above: Rugby football is the national game of Wales and Cardiff Arms Park is sacred ground to its devotees. When the Welsh supporters break into song the perfectly harmonized crescendo that sweeps through the stadium diminishes any challengers' hopes of gaining the triple crown.

Above: The steeply dropping Wye valley road from Monmouth to the south passes Tintern Abbey about halfway to Chepstow. The beauty of the Abbey's setting in lush green meadows beside the river, with tree-covered hills rising beyond, was an inspiration not only to William Wordsworth to write poetry – 'These waters, rolling from their mountain springs with a soft inland murmur' – but also to innumerable artists to paint this most romantic of scenes. Tintern is by no means a ruin in the ordinary sense of the word: the sight of sky above the roofless but otherwise remarkably whole abbey church adds greatly to its splendour as at Rievaulx, another Cistercian house. The nearby Anchor Inn is thought to have been the Abbey's water gate: a thirteenth century archway connects it with a slipway to the Wye.

more gently down to the Glamorgan coalfields. These coalfields, in their heyday, made Cardiff the greatest coal-exporting port in the world, but the years of depression in the 1920s taught her not to rely on heavy industries alone and today the city, which has been the capital of Wales since 20th December 1955, has varied industrial and commercial interests and is the cultural centre for the whole country.

South Wales is particularly proud of – and particularly concerned about – the Gower Peninsula. It is something of a miracle that this delectable area of headlands, sandy bays and open downs, so close to Swansea and Llanelli, was not overrun by its highly industrialized neighbours in the inconsiderate past. But thanks to the combined activities of the Wales Tourist Board, the National Trust (who have acquired or been given some 4665 acres (1900 hectares) in the peninsula); the Gower Society (a seemingly irresistible group of determined preservationists), and the Glamorgan County Naturalists'

Trust, its wild charm and beauty has been saved. But the very success of all this effort may yet be its undoing. What was once an inaccessible and unknown beauty spot is now attracting people in their thousands. The dilemma is how much human pressure can a beautiful but limited area take without losing its beauty.

Further to the west the equally beautiful Pembroke coast has, like the Brecon Beacons region, been declared a National Park. The 170-mile (273-km.) coastal path, which is the main artery of the Park, runs from St. Dogmaels, near Cardigan, to Amroth beyond Saundersfoot Bay. It also takes in the upper waters of Milford Haven and the islands of Caldy, Skokholm, Skomer, Grassholm and Ramsey.

As a tailpiece it is perhaps significant that nationalistic Wales is the home of one of the great experiments in international education – Atlantic College which occupies St. Donats Castle, magnificently situated on the coast between Porthcawl and Barry.

Above: The Wales Tourist Board's official guide to South Wales describes Three Cliffs Bay as 'a dreamy, sandy bay at the end of narrow lanes'. And 'dreamy' is a fair description of much of the spectacularly beautiful coastline of the Gower Peninsula. Though it is only a few miles from Swansea, Neath and Llanelli, the Peninsula manages to preserve its natural charm while enlarging its recreational attractions – a tribute to the firmness and foresight of the local authorities.

Left: Tenby is an ancient town that began to grow in the middle of the eighteenth century when John Jones, a local physician, promoted the virtues of sea water baths which the Tenby town fathers had established. New houses were built to accommodate the visiting gentry and the advent of the railway in 1853 further helped expansion. Though Tenby's position on a rocky headland on the western arm of Carmarthen Bay was chosen originally for its defensive strength, it perfectly fits the town's modern role of holiday resort as it provides two fine sandy beaches, one facing north and the other south.

NORTHERN IRELAND

IRELAND is one island and the six counties which make up the United Kingdom province of Northern Ireland are geographically part of that island. The division is so arbitrary that even the commonly used name of the province – Ulster – is imprecise. Historically Ulster includes Cavan, Donegal and Monaghan as well as the six counties of Antrim, Armagh, Down, Fermanagh, Londonderry and Tyrone. The border is there but the character and beauty of the landscape moves freely across it. The green hills are neither Catholic nor Protestant, neither Republican nor Loyalist.

Perhaps as much as anything it is the radiant beauty of this northern Irish countryside that accentuates the inter-denominational strife that the province has so long endured. Enmity is out of place in so welcoming a countryside. Away from Belfast or Londonderry the physical scars are relatively few and incidents, tragic as they are, seldom impinge on the life of country people. Indeed, many visitors find Northern Ireland

Above: Because of a disagreement in 1765, when Castleward, County Down, was built, the north front is in the Gothic style chosen by Lady Bangor while the south front is in the Palladian style favoured by Lord Bangor. The National Trust now owns both fronts and everything in between and opens the house to the public in the summer months.

Left: The Mountains of Mourne bring a lump to every Irishman's throat and no words can add to the evident beauty of this scene near Bryansford, County Down.

more peaceful than some of the world's more sought-after tourist areas.

The restful nature of the Irish scene has long been recognized. There is a special quality of light which tints the landscape a unique and unbelievable green, softens the outline of mountains, clarifies water and whitens the long, uncrowded beaches.

If events have not altered the countryside they have certainly not changed the people; they are still, by and large, the gentle, friendly, hospitable, relaxed men and women whose indifference to punctuality can sometimes be so infuriating to those who have trains to catch and appointments to keep.

Few capital cities can have easy access to so much beautiful countryside as Belfast has. You can go in any direction and encounter sights that are unique. To the north there are the mountains and glens of Antrim with the coast road literally within a stone's throw of the sea all the way from Larne to Cushendall – 25 miles (40 km.) of paradise – and then, near Portrush, nature's outsize experiment in crystallography: the Giant's Causeway. To the west is Lough Neagh, the largest lake in the British Isles and almost as full of legends as it is of water. To the south are the Mountains of Mourne which, as everyone knows and as every Irishman sings, sweep down to the sea. To the east Belfast Lough itself opens out like a great horn of plenty with the seaside resorts of Bangor and Carrickfergus on its shores and Mew Island at its entrance with one of the most powerful lighthouses in the world to guide ships down the 15-mile (24-km.) channel to Belfast.

Loughs are a prominent feature of the Northern Ireland countryside. Lough Neagh though large is shallow. It was formed, according to legend, when a giant scooped up a handful of mud to throw at his English enemy. The mud fell into the Irish Sea and formed the Isle of Man while the hole filled with water to form the lough. Five of the six counties share its shores and though stretches of its rim have become industrialized most has been left for the fishermen who harvest the eels and an unusual species of freshwater herring – the pollan. More picturesque, because it is a sea lough and tidal, is

Strangford Lough, almost totally land-locked except for a narrow entrance with the village of Strangford on one side and Portaferry on the other. The tides race between them with fantastic power. Most picturesque of all are the island-studded loughs of Upper and Lower Lough Erne in Co. Fermanagh, stretching some 30 miles (48 km.) from Belleek to Belturbet in Cavan, just over the Eire border. Londonderry (plain Derry in Northern Ireland), lying at the head of Lough Foyle, is the second largest city in the province and is certainly the city with the longest memory. Every year it commemorates the occasion in 1688 when 13 of the city's apprentices slammed shut the gates against the Catholic Earl of Antrim's regiment sent to capture the city by James II. Ever since, Londonderry has regarded itself as the guardian of Protestantism.

Above: Legend asserts that Finn MacCool, an Irish Giant, built the Giant's Causeway in order to cross to Scotland. Those less imaginative fellows, the geologists, dismiss this colourful theory and insist that it was formed when a huge sheet of molten basalt cooled several million years ago. Most of the pillars are six-sided but some are three-, seven-, eight- and even nine-sided. Surely only an Irish giant could have been so eccentric.

Above left: The Irish bar may not have the charm of its English counterpart, the village pub, but then drinking is a serious business in Ireland with a comparably high level of talk – and singing.

Right: Rathlin Island, seven miles (11 km.) off Ballycastle on the north-east tip of Ireland, is a paradise for the botanist, bird-watcher and fisherman. It is also the home of a farming and fishing community of around 100 people. It was in a cave on Rathlin that the exiled Robert Bruce admired the tenacity of the spider and, returning to Scotland to 'try, try again', triumphed at Bannockburn.

INDEX

ACKNOWLEDGMENTS
Malcolm Aird: 10 above, 10 below right, 34 left, 38 above, 51 above, 58 left, 89 below left; K. M. Andrew: 9, 15 above and below; Peter Baker: 12-13, 24-25, 73, 78 above, 83; The Sixth Marquess of Bath: 4-5; John Bethell: 29 above, 40 above right, 46, 52-53, 63, 89 above; James Betts: 20; British Tourist Authority: 11, 25, 28, 50 left, 52, 68, 80-81, 96; Camera and Pen International: 85 below; Colour Library International: 36, 37 below, 39, 56 below; Crown Copyright: reproduced by permission of Her Majesty's Stationery Office: 58-59; P. J. H. Halls: 66; Noel Habgood (Camera and Pen International): 1, 2-3, 8-9, 10 below left, 14, 16-17, 18 below, 19 below, 21, 22-23, 26-27, 32, 32-33, 66-67, 68-69, 74 above, 74-75, 76-77, 92-93; Robert Hallmann: 88; Michael Holford: 62 below; Angelo Hornak: 70-71; A. F. Kersting: 41, 70; Raymond Lea: 60, 62 above, 64 left, 65; National Trust: (John Bethell) 31 below, (Vernon Shaw) 45, (Andy Williams) 78 below; Northern Ireland Tourist Board: 93, 94 centre, 94-95; Picturepoint Ltd.: 26, 38 below, 46-47, 60-61, 64-65 above, 84, 86-87, 90-91, 91 below; Pix Photos Ltd.: (G. F. Allen) 40 below; John Rigby: 57 above, 59 above; Wilfrid Rolfe: 59 below right; Kenneth Scowen: back jacket, 18 above, 40 above left, 57 below, 73, 74 below; Brian Seed: 7; John Sims: 50 right, 64-65 below; Spectrum Colour Library: 23 inset, 54-55; Patrick Thurston: 34 above, 44; Bertram Unné: 31 above; Wales Tourist Board: 80, 82 above and below, 85 above, 86, 89 below right, 90; W. J. Webster: 13 above right; Jeremy Whitaker: 36 above, 71; Andy Williams: front jacket; Trevor Wood: end papers, 29 below left and right, 48, 49, 51 below, 67, 94 above; ZEF A: (F. A. H. Bloemendahl) 34-35; (H. J. Kreuger) 79; (F. Park) 30; (V. Phillips) 42-43.